Exploring
Computer Hardware

2024 Edition

Kevin Wilson

Elluminet Press
www.elluminetpress.com

Exploring Computer Hardware

Images used with permission. Wackerhausen, RainerKnäpper, KDS4444, monsitj, HLundgaard @ iStock. Mnyjhee @ Dreamstime. VIA Gallery from Hsintien, MikeRun, Danrok, Stockarch, Michael Gauthier, Luminescent Media / CC-BY-SA-3.0, 200 Degrees Pixabay, Andy Holmes, © Raimond Spekking

Publisher: Elluminet Press
Director: Kevin Wilson
Lead Editor: Steven Ashmore
Technical Reviewer: Mike Taylor, Robert Ashcroft
Copy Editors: Joanne Taylor, James Marsh
Proof Reader: Robert Ashcroft
Indexer: James Marsh
Cover Designer: Kevin Wilson

eBook versions and licenses are also available for most titles. Any supplementary material referenced by the author in this text is available to readers at

www.elluminetpress.com/resources

Table of Contents

About the Author

With over 20 years' experience in the computer industry, Kevin Wilson has made a career out of technology and showing others how to use it. After earning a master's degree in computer science, software engineering, and multimedia systems, Kevin has held various positions in the IT industry including graphic & web design, programming, building & managing corporate networks, and IT support.

He serves as senior writer and director at Elluminet Press Ltd, he periodically teaches computer science at college, and works as an IT trainer in England while researching for his PhD. His books have become a valuable resource among the students in England, South Africa, Canada, and in the United States.

Kevin's motto is clear: "If you can't explain something simply, then you haven't understood it well enough." To that end, he has created the Exploring Tech Computing series, in which he breaks down complex technological subjects into smaller, easy-to-follow steps that students and ordinary computer users can put into practice.

You can contact Kevin using his email address:

office@elluminetpress.com

Acknowledgements

Thanks to all the staff at Luminescent Media & Elluminet Press for their passion, dedication and hard work in the preparation and production of this book.

To all my friends and family for their continued support and encouragement in all my writing projects.

To all my colleagues, students and testers who took the time to test procedures and offer feedback on the book

Finally thanks to you the reader for choosing this book. I hope it helps you gain a better understanding of computer hardware.

The Computer

A computer is an electronic device that operates under the control of various programs. These programs, often referred to as software, enable a computer to perform a wide range of tasks.

A typical computer usually has a standard set of peripherals such as a keyboard, mouse and monitor. On a desktop computer, these peripherals are connected to a box that houses all the internal hardware, such as the CPU, RAM and Hard disks.

These days, there are many different types of computer, and they range from the smallest smart phone or tablet computer, to large super computers that fill entire buildings.

The most common ones you'll find are micro computers, built on the micro processor.

Have a look at the video demos to help you understand. Open your web browser and navigate to the following website:

elluminetpress.com/hw-cmp

On the back of a standard computer case, you'll find various ports. This is where the peripherals such as the printer, monitor, keyboard and mouse connect.

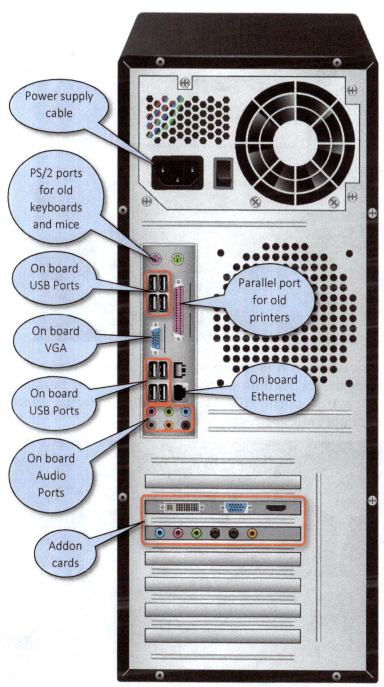

Chapter 1: The Computer

On the front of the case you'll usually find the power button. On some machines, you'll also find a few USB ports, a headphone jack and a card reader. You may also find a CD/DVD drive.

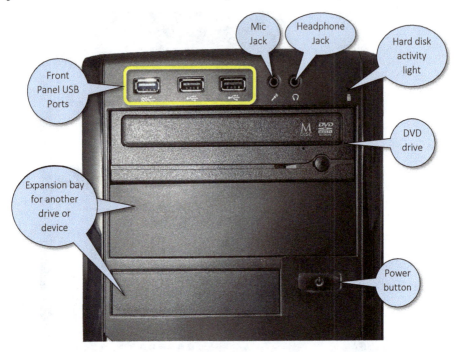

Laptops have various different ports scattered along the edges of the device depending on the model. On most laptops, you'll find a few USB ports, HDMI to connect an external monitor, an ethernet port and a headphone jack.

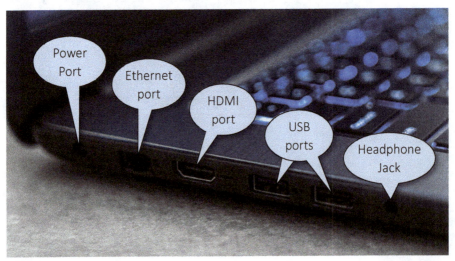

Basic Peripherals

The most common peripherals are:

- Monitors
- Printers
- Keyboards
- Mice
- Scanners
- Cameras

These are known as external peripherals, as they sit outside the case (the CPU), and connect to your computer via USB cable or similar. External peripherals can be divided into input devices or output devices.

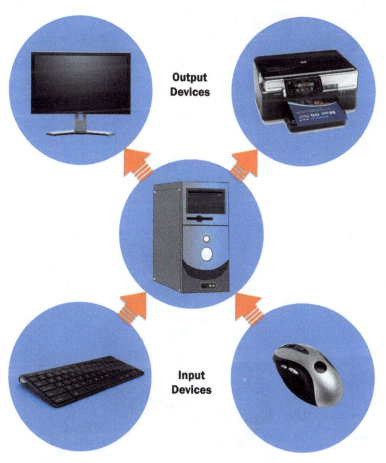

Output Devices

Input Devices

Other types of computer have similar peripherals, except they may be integrated into the device such as a laptop or tablet.

On a laptop, the keyboard, mouse/trackpad, and monitor are all integrated into the device - although you can attach these externally.

Similarly with a tablet. Although some peripherals are different, such as a touch screen instead of a mouse/trackpad. Also some tablets have external detachable keyboards.

Some tablets, have on-screen keyboards and some have limited data ports for additional peripherals.

These devices are designed for portability, so they only feature the essentials.

The Micro Computer

A microcomputer is a small, relatively inexpensive computer with a microprocessor that is commonly known as a Personal Computer. Personal computers nowadays come in various different forms depending on their function; desktops for higher performance, larger storage, more memory and bigger screens, or laptops and tablets for portability.

Desktop

The traditional desktop computer with a monitor, computer case, keyboard and mouse. Can either be a Mac or a PC.

These machines are usually larger and offer the highest levels of computing power. They are aimed at gamers, graphic designers, video editors, office users, and other professional users. They are well suited to large screens, high performance, and ample storage space.

Desktop computer sales for home users have been steadily declining in favour of laptops and tablet computers.

Desktop computers still seem to have a place in an office environment, however this seems to be slowly changing toward a cloud based environment where data is stored on the cloud and accessed using laptops or tablets.

Desktop: All-in-one

This type of desktop is virtually identical to the traditional desktop we talked about above, except the computer case has been done away with.

Instead, all the internal hardware (processor, RAM, hard disc and video card) from the computer case, is integrated into the back of the screen itself.

This makes the whole system easier to set up, as all you need to do is plug in your keyboard and mouse, hook it up to the power and you're ready to go.

Some of these systems have touch screens built in, allowing you to tap icons on the screen instead of using a mouse.

Apple's iMac popularised this format, and many other manufacturers have copied the design.

Laptop

A typical laptop computer, also sometimes called a notebook. This one is a laptop running Windows 10.

Laptops usually have a similar spec to their desktop counterparts, however there are some compromises due to space. They tend to have less RAM and run slightly slower than desktops. The screens are usually between 12" and 17".

They can run all the software and apps that are available on a desktop and come with Windows 10/11 or MacOS.

The major advantage of a laptop, it its portability. The fact that you can use it in any room, sit on the sofa and surf the web, talk to your friends. Or do some college work in a coffee shop or library.

With laptops, you can plug in various peripherals such as a mouse as well as an external screen or projector. This makes them ideal for those who do public speaking, teaching/lecturing, and presentation.

Some laptops nowadays even include touch screens where you can navigate around the screen by tapping icons and menus rather than using a mouse or trackpad.

Netbook

Netbooks are small cut down versions of laptops. They have less RAM, HDD space and are designed to be small, lightweight and inexpensive which makes them great for carrying around.

The screens are usually about 10". Notice the size compared to the ball point pen in the photograph.

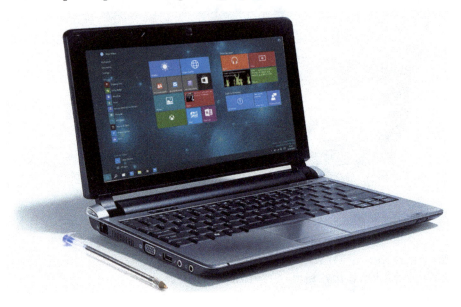

Netbooks can run Windows 10/11, some form of Linux or even Chrome OS.

These are great for working on the go or travelling around. They can run traditional software such as Microsoft Office and work well when browsing the web, social media or keeping in touch via email.

These have limited power, so anything more processor intensive such as Creative Suite or some types of games will struggle to run on these machines.

These machines also have limited storage space, so if you have a lot of music, documents, videos, or photographs, you'll quite quickly run out of space.

Most of these machines can be used with some kind of cloud storage such as OneDrive or GoogleDrive.

Chromebook

A ChromeBook is a laptop or tablet that runs an operating system called Chrome OS and uses Google's Chrome Web Browser to run web apps.

At its core, Chrome OS is a Linux based operating system and will run on hardware with either Intel/AMD x86/64 or ARM processors.

Chromebooks are designed to be used mainly online, meaning they work best when connected to the internet at home, in the office, at school, college, the library, or while out and about. Without an internet connection, a Chromebook can still function, but its features and available applications are more limited.

Traditional desktop software such as Microsoft Office, Adobe Creative Suite and many types of games do not run on these machines. However, Google have developed their own alternatives, and Adobe and Microsoft have released web based versions of their software.

You can also download countless apps from the Google Play Store for all your other software needs from social media and communication, to getting your work done.

Tablet Computers

Tend to be a cut down compact version designed with touch screens. This one is running Windows 10 in desktop mode.

Examples of these come in the form of iPad, Microsoft Surface Tablets, Surface Tablets, Samsung Galaxy Tab, Amazon Fire and many more.

These are ideal for travelling and carrying about as they are light weight and can be stored in your bag easily.

They have countless apps available from the app store that you can download directly onto your tablet. These range from games to cut down versions of Microsoft Office and basic graphics packages. They are also good for browsing the web, social media, making video calls and keeping in touch using email.

Some tablets can even run traditional software, if they are running Windows 10/11.

Hybrids

Hybrids are a cross between laptop computers and tablets. An example of a hybrid is Microsoft's surface tablet.

These can function as a laptop and have detachable keyboards. Once you detach the keyboard you can use the device in tablet mode, attach the keyboard and you can use it as a laptop.

These devices aren't usually as powerful as traditional laptops and are usually smaller and light weight.

They also have countless apps available from the app store that you can download directly onto your hybrid. These range from games to cut down versions of Microsoft Office and basic graphics packages. They are also good for browsing the web, social media, making video calls and keeping in touch using email.

Some hybrids can even run traditional software, if they run Windows 10/11.

Macs and PCs

There are primarily two categories of personal computers available to in most stores: Apple Macs and Windows-based PCs. The fundamental difference between choosing a Mac or a PC lies in the operating system and the surrounding hardware ecosystem. Macs typically have a higher entry-level price than many PCs, although prices vary significantly in both categories. Premium, high-performance PCs can be just as expensive as high-end Macs, while some Macs are positioned as relatively affordable options. As a result, the decision often depends on budget, performance requirements, personal preference, and how the computer will be used.

macOS runs many common applications used for everyday tasks, creative work, and software development. However, Windows has a larger user base, especially in businesses and technical industries. Because of this, many specialist programs, older legacy applications, and industry-specific tools are more commonly developed for Windows. As a result, users who rely on particular professional or niche software are more likely to find it available on a Windows PC, while macOS users generally have access to most mainstream and modern applications.

It is often assumed that Macs are primarily intended for creative professionals, such as graphic designers or video editors, but this is not exclusively the case.

It is often assumed that Macs are primarily intended for creative professionals, such as graphic designers or video editors, but this is not exclusively the case. Macs and PCs are both widely used in creative industries, and many high-end Windows systems are specifically designed to handle demanding creative workloads. At the same time, Macs are increasingly common in business and professional environments, supported by strong productivity tools and full compatibility with widely used office software.

Gaming is an area where Windows PCs generally maintain an advantage, largely due to greater hardware flexibility and a much larger catalogue of supported games. Customisable graphics cards, driver support, and long-standing developer focus make PCs the preferred choice for many gamers. Although gaming on Macs has improved in recent years, it still remains more limited compared to the Windows platform.

Ultimately, both Macs and PCs are capable of supporting a wide range of everyday and professional tasks. Activities such as document creation, internet use, media consumption, photo editing, and communication can be handled effectively by either platform. For many users, the choice comes down to personal preference, required software, hardware flexibility, and budget.

Mainframe Computer

Mainframe computers are high-performance machines that excel in large-scale, intensive processing. They are often used for complex, critical applications such as bulk data processing, census records processing, statistical computations, enterprise resource planning, and transaction processing for large institutions like banks and government entities.

They are known for their high speed, exceptional reliability, robust security, scalability, and the ability to support numerous peripherals and concurrent users — often in the thousands or even tens of thousands. With their powerful processing capabilities and large memory capacity, mainframes are designed to handle vast amounts of data and computation.

Mainframes usually occupy large spaces, sometimes an entire room or a floor of a building, due to their size and the peripheral equipment associated with them. However, modern mainframes have significantly reduced in size without compromising their performance capabilities, although they are still much larger than the typical server or personal computer.

Due to their design and capabilities, mainframes have high up-time and are often used in environments where system availability is paramount. They come with redundant hardware components and sophisticated software failover capabilities to ensure they continue to run even if some of their components fail.

Lastly, despite the advent and proliferation of cloud computing, mainframes still have a significant presence in certain industries and applications, where they continue to offer a level of performance and reliability that is challenging to match.

Super Computer

A supercomputer is a computer system that has extremely high processing capabilities, making it capable of processing large amounts of data and performing complex calculations.

These machines are designed to be extremely fast and efficient, often using parallel processing techniques to execute many trillions of operations simultaneously. They can consist of thousands or even millions of processors.

Blue Gene is a series of supercomputers designed by IBM, with various models having different numbers of processors and processing capabilities. This particular model in the photo below has over 250,000 processors capable of performing hundreds of trillions of operations per second. These processors are housed in multiple cabinets typically interconnected via a high-speed optical network. Due to the immense amount of heat they generate, these machines require air conditioning to maintain optimal operating temperatures.

Supercomputers play a vital role in the field of computational science and are used for a wide range of processor intensive tasks. They are also used in quantum mechanics, weather forecasting, and climate research where very large amounts of data need to be processed quickly and accurately.

Embedded Systems

An embedded system is a small computer designed for a specific purpose and is usually embedded into the device it controls. The computer program is usually stored either in ROM or some kind of flash memory and is known as firmware. These systems can be embedded into digital cameras, smart phones, cars, and household devices such as DVD players, washing machines, microwaves and smart TVs.

Decoding the Jargon

In this section, we'll take a look at come common computer and peripheral specifications you might find online or when shopping for a computer.

Computer Specs

Understanding these terms before shopping for a computer can be quite helpful. I have tried to filter out the unnecessary technical jargon and highlight the information that's most important.

The key components to pay attention to are the processor (CPU), graphics card (GPU), hard drive (storage), and RAM (memory).

The processor or CPU (Central Processing Unit) is essentially the brain of the computer. It performs most of the processing inside the computer. The speed and number of cores in the CPU will greatly affect the computer's performance.

The graphics card or GPU (Graphics Processing Unit) is particularly important if you plan on using your computer for tasks that require a lot of graphical power such as video editing, graphic design, or gaming.

The hard drive is where all your data is stored. This includes everything from your operating system to your documents and photos. Today, many computers use solid-state drives (SSD) which are faster and more reliable than traditional hard disk drives (HDD). Don't confuse this with memory (RAM).

RAM (Random Access Memory) is the short-term memory of the computer. It temporarily stores data that the CPU uses, helping your computer process information faster. More RAM generally means a smoother experience when running multiple applications at the same time.

Most modern machines come with a built-in WiFi connection as well as a keyboard and mouse. However, always double-check what's included.

Printer Specs

When you're shopping for a printer, there are several important specifications to consider:

Print Speed: This is usually measured in pages per minute (ppm). Higher print speed is beneficial for high volume printing.

Print Quality: For standard text documents, most printers will do an adequate job. If you plan on printing high-quality photos or graphics, you'll want a printer with a high print resolution, which is measured in dots per inch (dpi). The higher the dpi, the better the print quality.

Color or Monochrome: If you only need to print text documents, a monochrome (black and white) printer may be all you need. However, if you need to print photos or color documents, you'll need a color printer.

Type of Printer: The two most common types of printers are inkjet and laser. Inkjet printers are typically less expensive upfront and can print both text documents and high-quality photos. Laser printers are generally more cost-effective for fast, high-volume printing.

Connectivity: Printers can connect to your computer via USB, Ethernet (wired), or WiFi (wireless). Some newer models also support mobile printing technologies like Apple's AirPrint or Google Cloud Print.

Ink/Toner: Printers use either ink (for inkjet printers) or toner (for laser printers). Some printers have a single cartridge for all colors, while others have separate cartridges for each color.

Computer Software

Although this is a book on computer hardware, it's worth noting that the hardware is useless without software. So let's take a brief look at the different types of computer software that make a computer work.

Computer software comes in a variety of different forms: Applications, Utilities, and System Software.

Application software is designed to perform specific tasks or activities. This includes a broad spectrum of applications such as word processors, web browsers, multimedia players, and business applications.

Utilities are small programs that are designed to configure, analyse, optimise or maintain a computer, such as antivirus, scandisc or defrag.

System software is designed to operate and control the hardware of a computer system, providing a necessary platform for application software. It includes the operating systems and device drivers.

Device Drivers

Device drivers are specialized software programs that allow the computer's operating system to communicate with and control hardware devices such as printers, video cards, network adapters, keyboards and mice.

Operating Systems

As well as all the hardware and peripherals, you need software to make the computer work. The first piece of software that is needed is called an Operating System.

This could be:

- Windows 10, Windows 11 or Linux
- MacOS if you're on a Mac Computer
- ChromeOS if you're using a ChromeBook
- iPadOS if you're using an iPad
- Or Android if you're using a tablet

Here we can see Windows 11 running on a PC and MacOS running on a Mac.

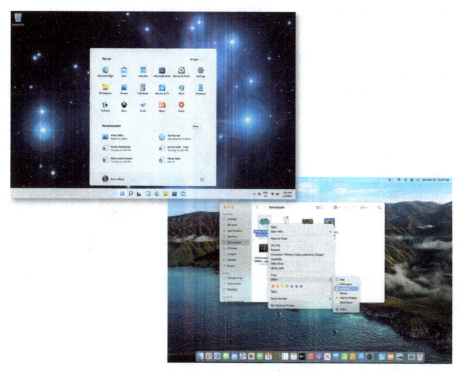

Another operating system you might come across is Linux. Many tech enthusiasts and privacy-focused users prefer Linux for its security features and open-source nature, which allows them to customize the operating systems to suit their needs. Many companies also use Linux for developing and running applications, servers, and databases.

Linux comes in various distributions, or "distros," such as Ubuntu, Fedora, Centos, and Debian. These package the Linux kernel with a variety of software applications to meet different needs.

Chapter 1: The Computer

Here in the image below, we can see iOS running on an iPhone. The iPhone's Operating system allows the user to interact with the system by tapping on icons rather than using a mouse.

As you can see, the Operating System provides a user interface where you can use various tools called programs or software to do your work.

For example, Microsoft Office is a software application package that allows you to create documents, presentations, spreadsheets and so on. Photoshop is a program for editing photos.

Apps and Applications

Applications are pieces of software that can be quite large and were originally designed to run on a desktop computer; you use the application using a keyboard and mouse. These are known as desktop apps or applications. Examples include Microsoft Office Suite: Word, Excel, PowerPoint, as well as Adobe Creative Suite: Photoshop, Adobe Premiere and so on.

On the setup below, we have Microsoft Word running on an all in one desktop computer.

You interact with the system using a keyboard and mouse, so the application and its interface is designed with this in mind. This is an example of a desktop application. This application could also be running on a laptop.

32

A more recent incarnation is the Mobile App. These are software applications designed to run on smartphones, tablets, and other mobile devices. Examples include social media apps such as Facebook and Instagram, productivity apps such as Google Docs, and Google Maps.

These Mobile Apps are usually smaller in size and are designed with a touch screen in mind.

In the demo below, we have a maps app running on a tablet.

You interact with the system using your finger to manipulate the screen directly using a number of finger gestures; point, drag, tap etc. The interface is designed with this in mind, making icons bigger to enable you to tap on them with your finger.

The terms "app" and "application" are often used interchangeably, but they do carry a subtle difference.

Application is the full term and refers to any software program designed to perform a specific function for the user or another application. The term is often used to describe more complex software such as Microsoft Office, Adobe Creative Suite, or database systems that run in a desktop/keyboard/mouse environment (ie a desktop application).

Chapter 1: The Computer

App typically refers to software applications that are designed for mobile devices such as smartphones and tablets. Apps are generally smaller in scale than full desktop applications, and are downloaded from app stores such as Google Play, Microsoft Store, or the Apple App Store, depending on what platform the app is running on.

Utilities

Utilities are small programs that are designed to configure, analyse, optimise or maintain a computer, such as antivirus, scandisk or defrag. These tools vary widely in function and include:

Antivirus Utilities protect the computer from malware, viruses, and cyber threats. Windows Security for example, is an antivirus suite that is built into Microsoft Windows and provides real-time protection against threats. Others include Avast and AVG antivirus.

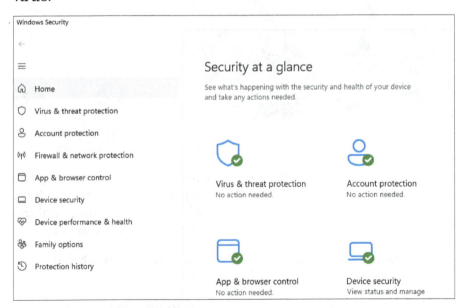

Disk Management Utilities such as scandisk (chkdsk) and defrag optimize the data on a hard disk drive. Scandisk (chkdsk) checks the disk for errors and repairs file systems, while defragmentation tools (defrag) rearrange fragmented data to improve disk performance.

System Monitoring Utilities monitor system resources such as CPU usage, memory usage, and disk activity. They provide crucial insights into how the system resources are being used and help identify bottlenecks or other issues.

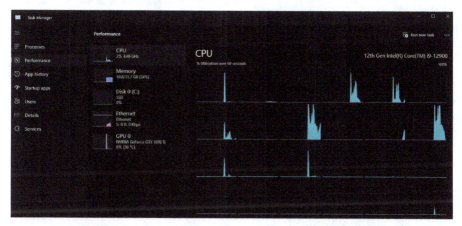

Backup Utilities ensure data continuity by creating copies of data that can be restored in case of a data loss event. These tools can automate the backup process and can often restore systems to their previous state.

Network Utilities are used in setting up, managing, and troubleshooting of network connections. These include programs such as network monitors, and Wi-Fi analyzers.

File Management Utilities such as File Explorer in Windows allow you to organize, search, and manage files and folders.

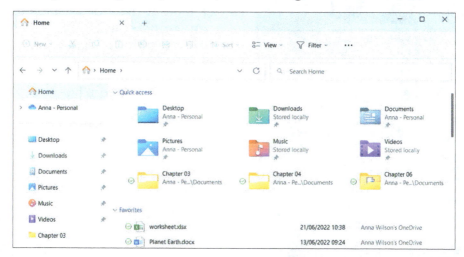

2

Hardware Components

Computer systems are made up of various different hardware components such as a central processor (CPU), memory (RAM), storage space (HDD) and so on. This is called internal hardware and usually plugs into a main board called a motherboard.

Devices that sit outside are called peripherals and include printers, scanners, keyboards, mice, cameras and so on.

There is also removable storage such as memory cards, USB sticks and external hard drives that are designed to be portable.

Have a look at the video demos to help you understand. Open your web browser and navigate to the following website:

`elluminetpress.com/hw-dev`

Types of Hardware

On a desktop computer, the case houses all the internal hardware. Peripherals sit outside the case - this is known as external hardware.

Internal Hardware

Internal hardware refers to hardware components that are inside the computer's case. Such as the CPU or processor, main memory (RAM), the hard disk drive, and a graphics card.

These are all mounted onto a main circuit board called a motherboard.

External Peripherals

The most common peripherals are

- Monitors

- Printers

- Keyboards

- Mice

- Scanners

- Cameras

These all sit outside the case and connect to your computer via USB cable or similar.

Some familiar ones are pictured below. Here, you have a computer monitor and printer. These are sometimes called output devices.

A keyboard and mouse used on standard PCs, laptops, servers and so on. These are sometimes called input devices.

Primary Storage Devices

Primary storage, also known as main memory, or internal memory, is memory that is accessed directly by the CPU.

Random Access Memory (RAM)

Computer memory or main memory, commonly known as RAM (Random Access Memory), primarily consists of silicon chips mounted on removable modules called DIMMs (Dual Inline Memory Modules). RAM serves as the computer's primary workspace, temporarily holding software instructions and data that the CPU needs to access quickly. This type of memory is categorized as volatile, which means it requires a continuous power source to maintain data integrity. When the power supply is interrupted, all data stored in volatile memory is lost.

For example if you are typing a document in Microsoft Word, both Microsoft Word and your document are loaded into and stored in the computer's memory while you are working on it. This is not to be confused with the Hard Disk.

DRAM

The first type of RAM we'll take a look at is DRAM. DRAM stands for Dynamic Random Access Memory and is the memory used to store data in personal computers.

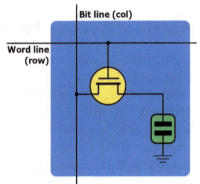

DRAM stores each bit of information in a cell composed of a capacitor and a transistor. The transistor admits current to the capacitor during writes, and discharges the capacitor during reads.

If there is a charge in the capacitor, it is read as a 1, if there is no charge, it is read as a 0.

The capacitor in a DRAM cell can hold a charge for only a few milliseconds, and is said to be 'dynamic', because the cell must be constantly recharged (or refreshed) in order to retain its data.

SDRAM

The next type of RAM is called SDRAM (or synchronous DRAM). This type of DRAM is called synchronous because its operation is synchronized with an external clock signal (such as the computer's internal clock). SDRAM uses only the rising edge of the clock signal to transfer data.

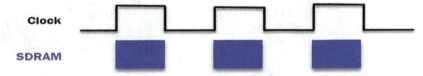

DDR SDRAM

DDR stands for Double Data Rate and is a memory technology that works by allowing operations to occur on both the rising and falling edge of the clock cycle, thereby effectively doubling the data rate without increasing the clock frequency.

Reading and Writing Data

The data is stored in memory cells arranged in a grid like pattern called a memory array. The rows are called wordlines and the columns are called bitlines. Each memory array can contain thousands of cells or even millions, but to simplify the design so we can understand what's going on, we'll use an 8x8 memory array.

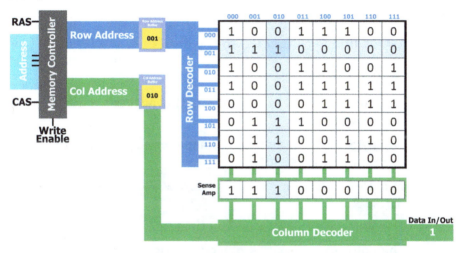

Let's take a look at what each part of the diagram does.

Memory Controller manages the flow of data to and from the DRAM. It generates the addresses and control signals required to access the memory cells.

Address Bus carries the address signals that specify the row and column of the memory cell to be accessed.

Row Address Buffer temporarily holds the row address.

Column Address Buffer temporarily holds the column address.

Row Decoder decodes the row address from the buffer and activates the corresponding row line in the memory matrix.

Column Decoder decodes the column address from the buffer and activates the corresponding column line in the memory matrix.

Memory Array is a grid of memory cells where data is stored. Each cell can hold a bit of data (0 or 1).

41

Chapter 2: Hardware Components

Sense Amplifier reads the data from the selected memory cell.

RAS (Row Address Strobe) activates the row address buffer to latch the row address.

CAS (Column Address Strobe) activates the column address buffer to latch the column address.

Write Enable indicates whether the operation is a read or a write.

Data In/Out line is connected to the data bus.

During a read cycle:

1. The row address is placed on the address pins via the address bus.
2. The RAS pin is activated. This places the row address into the Row Address Buffer.
3. The Row Decoder selects the row which is sent to the Sense Amp.
4. The Write Enable pin is deactivated.
5. The column address is placed on the address pins via the address bus.
6. The CAS pin is activated. This places the column address into the Column Address Buffer.
7. The Column Decoder selects the data from the selected column in the Sense Amp, and places it on the Data Out pin, which is connected to the data bus.
8. Refresh row with data from Sense Amp.
9. The RAS and CAS pins are both deactivated and the cycle begins again.

During a write cycle:

1. The row address is placed on the address pins via the address bus.
2. The RAS pin is activated. This places the row address into the Row Address Buffer.
3. The Row Decoder selects the row which is sent to the Sense Amp.

4. The input value placed on the Data In pin, then the Write Enable pin is activated.

5. The column address is placed on the address pins via the address bus.

6. The CAS pin is activated. This places the column address into the Column Address Buffer.

7. The value from the Data In pin is loaded into the Sense Amp according to column address.

8. Refresh row (with the modified data from Sense Amp).

9. The RAS and CAS pins are both deactivated and the cycle begins again.

A single memory array would just store and retrieve one bit of data. To store a byte, we would need an 8 of these arrays.

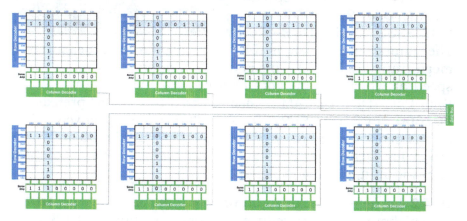

During a read/write cycle, the same row and column is selected in each array. The selected bit from each array is output onto its data in/out pin. The data in/out pin on each memory array makes up one line on the data bus.

A DRAM chip is divided internally into banks. A 'bank' is one of several separate memory arrays inside the chip, each with its own row-selection and reading circuits.

A rank is built from multiple DRAM chips working together, and each of those chips contains its own set of banks, so a single rank encompasses many banks indirectly through its member chips.

DDR is a refinement of the earlier SDRAM technology and offers higher speeds by transferring data on both the rising and falling edges of the clock signal, effectively doubling the data rate without increasing the clock frequency as introduced on page 40.

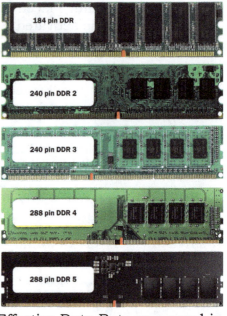

DDR, also known as DDR1, was introduced around 2000 and marked a significant advance over traditional SDRAM by doubling the data transfer rate. Standard speeds include **DDR-200**, **DDR-266**, **DDR-333**, and **DDR-400**. The number after 'DDR' is the Effective Data Rate measured in mega-transfers (MT/s). This is usually double the internal clock speed at which the memory operates. Hence the term Double Data Rate. DDR SDRAM is also referred to with PC prefixes as **PC1600**, **PC2100**, **PC2700**, and **PC3200** respectively. This means peak transfer rates of 1600 MB/s for DDR-200 and 3200 MB/s for DDR-400. The "PC" prefix signifies the theoretical bandwidth in megabytes per second.

DDR2 launched in 2003, brought enhancements over **DDR1** with higher speeds and reduced power consumption at 1.8 volts. Standard speeds are **DDR2-400**, **DDR2-533**, **DDR2-667**, and **DDR2-800**. These are referred to with PC prefixes as **PC2-3200**, **PC2-4200**, **PC2-5300**, and **PC2-6400** respectively, with peak bandwidths of 3200 MB/s for **DDR2-400** and 6400 MB/s for **DDR2-800**.

DDR3 launched in 2007, represents a further enhancement in terms of power efficiency and performance. **DDR3** operates at a reduced voltage of 1.5 volts. Speeds range from **DDR3-800** to **DDR3-1600**, with corresponding PC prefixes indicating their theoretical bandwidths: **DDR3-800** is known as **PC3-6400**, at 6400 MB/s; **DDR3-1066** as **PC3-8500** at 8500 MB/s; **DDR3-1333** as **PC3-10600** at 10600 MB/s; and **DDR3-1600** as **PC3-12800,** which runs at 12800 MB/s.

DDR4 the standard since 2014, advances the technology even further with higher speeds, increased density, and lower voltage requirements at 1.2 volts. Speeds begin at **DDR4-2133** up to **DDR4-3200**. These are labelled accordingly with PC prefixes such as **PC4-17000** for **DDR4-2133** indicating a bandwidth of 17,000 MB/s, **PC4-19200** for **DDR4-2400** at 19,200 MB/s, and **PC4-25600** for **DDR4-3200** at 25,600 MB/s.

DDR5 introduced around 2020, enhances data transfer efficiency, capacity, and power management even further while operating at a nominal voltage of 1.1 volts. The industry uses the PC prefix less often in consumer contexts. Instead, the naming focuses on the **DDR5** designation followed by the effective data rate. For example **DDR5-4800** indicates an effective data rate of transfers near 4800 MT/s.

Laptops have their own type of memory. It's more or less the same except for the physical size. These memory modules are called SO-DIMMs

SRAM

Static Random Access Memory (SRAM) is a type of semiconductor memory that uses bistable latching circuitry to store each bit of data. Each SRAM cell typically consists of four to six transistors (or MOSFETs) that form a flip-flop, capable of maintaining a stable state of 0 or 1 as long as power is supplied. This configuration allows SRAM to retain data without the need for refresh cycles as in DRAM/SDRAM, which requires periodic recharging of its capacitors to retain data.

SRAM is faster than DRAM/SDRAM due to its transistor-based design, which enables quicker access to stored data. The absence of refresh cycles contributes to this speed, as the memory cell is always ready to be read or written to, without the delay associated with recharging capacitors in DRAM/SDRAM.

This makes SRAM suitable for applications where speed is critical, such as in cache memory.

Cache Memory

The cache is usually an extremely fast SRAM memory chip that stores data so that subsequent requests for that data can be served faster.

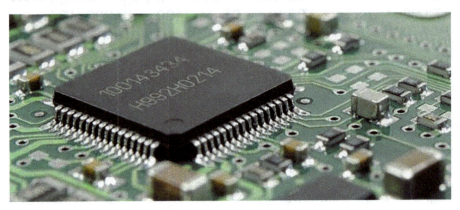

For example, data read from a hard disk drive can be stored in a cache, so when a program requests that data again, it can be read from the cache instead of from the hard disk drive.

Read Only Memory (ROM)

Read Only Memory is non-volatile memory or storage containing data that cannot be changed.

Read Only Memory is useful for storing a program that very rarely change. An example is the BIOS program needed to start a PC, sometimes known as firmware.

Secondary Storage

Secondary storage, also known as auxiliary storage is memory that is used to permanently store computer software and data. This type of memory is known as non-volatile memory as it can retain the data even when the power is turned off. Non-volatile memory is used for permanent storage and backup.

When you install an Operating System, an application, or save a file, these are stored on a secondary storage device such as a hard disk drive.

Secondary storage devices are divided into three types: magnetic, solid state, and optical.

- Magnetic storage devices such as hard disk drives use a magnetic field to magnetise sections of the disk to store data. These devices tend to be large in capacity and cheap.

- Solid state devices use flash memory to store data. These devices tend to be small in capacity, expensive, and are fast.

- Optical devices use a laser to read data from a CD, DVD or Bluray disk. You can also write data to a disk, however this is usually permanent and can't be erased.

Secondary storage devices are usually connected to the motherboard using a SATA cable. Here you can see the hard disk drive on the right with the SATA cable leading to a SATA port on the motherboard.

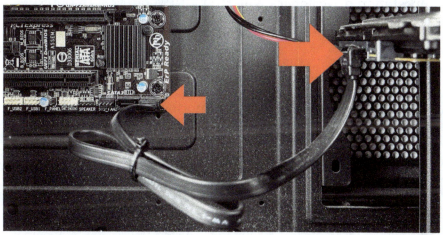

Hard Disk Drive (HDD)

The hard disk drive, also known as a hard drive, functions in a similar fashion to a filing cabinet, as it permanently stores all your documents, photographs, music, as well as your operating system (such as Microsoft Windows) and installed software (such as Microsoft Word).

When you launch an application like Microsoft Word, the software is retrieved from the hard disk and loaded into the computer's main memory, or RAM. This allows you to access and work on your documents.

These drives are called internal drives as they live inside the computer's case. The drive must first be formatted by the Operating System before it can store data. PCs use 3.5" drives, while laptops use smaller 2.5" drives.

Hard disks typically have storage capacities measured in gigabytes (GB) or terabytes (TB), with common sizes ranging from 500GB to 4+TB. Most modern hard disk drives (HDDs) operate at a speed of 7200 revolutions per minute (RPM), facilitating faster data access and file transfers. However, less expensive drives may run at 5400RPM, which might result in slower performance on modern computers. Some high-performance server and workstation drives operate at 10,000RPM or even 15,000RPM.

These drives connect to the computer's motherboard via a cable.

SATA is the most common interface used in modern personal computers for connecting hard drives.

SCSI (Small Computer System Interface) is generally used in servers and specialized workstations for tasks that require high performance and reliability.

SAS (Serial Attached SCSI) combine the robustness and reliability SCSI with a serial architecture similar to SATA. SAS is used in enterprise environments for its greater speed, scalability, and reliability.

Inside the hard drive, you'll see a stack of double sided disk platters with an actuator arm containing a electromagnetic read/write head that hovers microns above the surface of the disk.

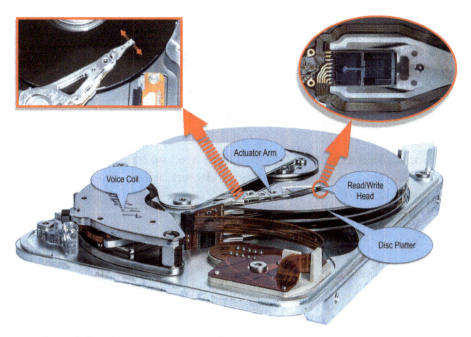

As the disk platters rotate, the actuator arm moves back and forth positioning the head on the correct track/sector of the disk in order to read or write data.

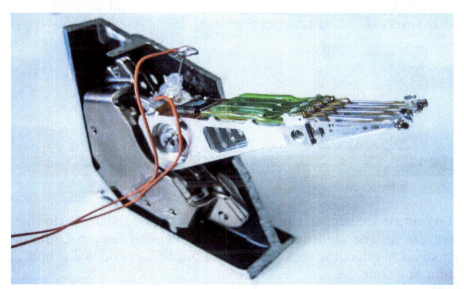

The read/write head on the end of the actuator arm is an electromagnet that hovers microns above the surface of the disk. An electro magnet is essentially a length of insulated wire wound around an iron core. A voltage is then applied to the wire.

This produces a magnetic field. There are two magnetic polarities: South-North and North-South, as shown below. Each magnetic field is called a flux.

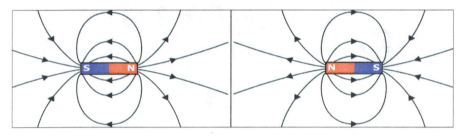

The binary data can be encoded by switching the polarity of the magnetic field (by reversing the current on the electro magnet). This is known as a flux reversal. The drive head detects these flux reversals when reading the data.

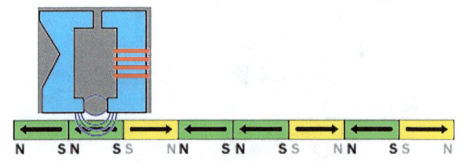

So how do we encode the binary data onto the HDD? To do this, we use an encoding scheme (for example Run Length Limited). Instead of encoding each individual bit, RLL encodes a group of bits at a time.

Data is stored using runs that are unique patterns of 1s and 0s. The run length is the number of consecutive 0s before a 1 is recorded.

For example, RLL (2,7) has run length minimum of 2 and maximum of 7. This means that the smallest number of spaces between flux reversals is 2, and the largest number of flux reversals is 7. The 'R' in the table means a flux reversal. 'N' means no flux reversal.

	Bit Pattern	Encoding
1	11	RNNN
2	10	NRNN
3	011	NNRNNN
4	010	RNNRNN
5	000	NNNRNN
6	0010	NNRNNRNN
7	0011	NNNNRNNN

If we were writing the following byte to the hard disk:

00001110

We can encode this using the table opposite. The first three 0s in the byte match the fifth bit pattern: 000

Next we have 011, then finally 10

So we have these three bit patterns: 000-011-10

	Bit Pattern	Encoding
1	11	RNNN
2	10	NRNN
3	011	NNRNNN
4	010	RNNRNN
5	000	NNNRNN
6	0010	NNRNNRNN
7	0011	NNNNRNNN

We can see this by matching up the bit patterns in the table. If we look across the table:

000 is encoded as NNN**R**NN
011 is encoded as NN**R**NNN
10 is encoded as N**R**NN

		Bit Pattern	Encoding
5		000	NNNRNN
3		011	NNRNNN
2		10	NRNN

So, on the hard disk, this would be written as:

NNNRNN**NNRNNN**NRNN

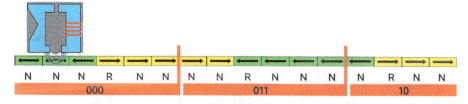

Modern hard disks do not use Run Length Limited (RLL) encoding anymore. Instead, they use more advanced encoding methods that allow for higher data density and faster performance.

Solid State Drive (SSD)

These drives perform much like a traditional Hard Disk but are extremely fast and also expensive. SSDs have no moving parts and are composed of non-volatile NAND flash memory, which is a type of memory that retains data even if the power is turned off.

There are various types of SSD drive available. The first type is the **SATA SSD**. This drive looks similar to a traditional hard disk drive (HDD) and plugs into the same SATA interface.

Next is the **M.2 SATA SSD drive.** These drives look like this:

M.2 is a form factor for small internal expansion cards. Notice the two notches on the card connector on the right (Key B & M).

These are older SSDs that still use the AHCI SATA Interface. The AHCI SATA storage interface has been superseded by NVMe.

NVMe M.2 or Non-Volatile Memory Express is a new high-speed storage protocol using PCI Express (x4) that was designed especially for SSDs. Drives that support this protocol have only one notch on the M.2 card connector (Key M).

In order to make use of one of these drives, your PC's motherboard will need to have an M.2 slot. An M.2 slot will look something like this:

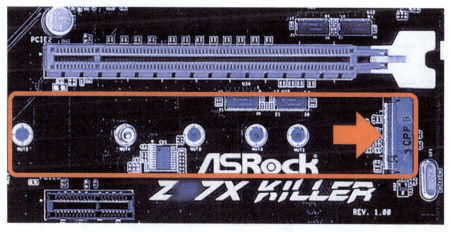

The M.2 drive plugs into the slot and lies flat along the motherboard.

These drives are being used in smaller laptops/notebook computers and on some tablet computers where you don't require large amounts of storage space.

SSDs give a tremendous speed boost to the computer, allowing applications to start up in seconds, as well as allowing the operating system to start much quicker than with a traditional hard disk drive (HDD).

RAID

RAID stands for Redundant Array of Independent Disks and is a data storage virtualization technology that combines multiple hard disk drives into a storage array for the purposes of data redundancy, performance, or both. There are various RAID levels.

RAID 0 data is striped across two or more disks to increase performance. This setup provides no fault tolerance, if one drive fails all the data is lost.

The data is split into blocks, and distributed across the disks.

RAID 1 usually consists of two drives. Data is written to one drive then mirrored (copied) to the second drive.

This setup provides fault tolerance, if one drive fails the data is recoverable from the second drive.

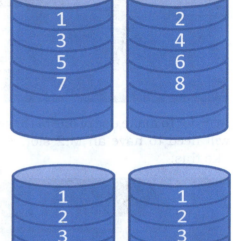

RAID 5 usually uses three or more drives. The data is striped across the drives with parity check. This provides both performance and fault tolerance.

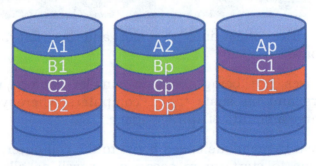

If a drive fails, the data can be reconstructed using the parity data.

RAID 10, also known as RAID 1+0, is a RAID configuration that combines disk mirroring (RAID 1) and disk striping (RAID 0) to protect data. RAID 10 requires a minimum of 4 drives.

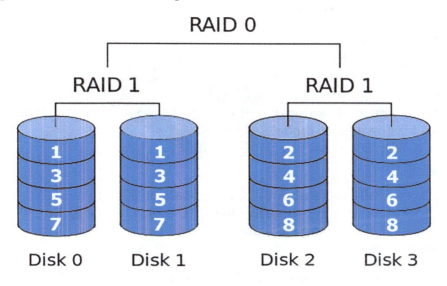

This is known as a nested RAID. As you can see, the two RAID 1 arrays are nested into a RAID 0 array.

RAID 5 arrays are often used in servers such as a web servers and data servers where there is a good trade off between data redundancy and performance.

Write operations can be slow because of the need to write the parity data, but read times are very fast.

Here on the right is a RAID 5 array with four hard disks installed in a web server. This particular RAID uses 4 SATA drives all connected to a RAID controller on the server's motherboard.

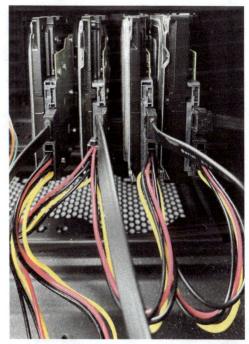

CD/DVD/Blu-ray Drive

CDs (Compact Disks), DVDs (Digital Versatile Disks), and Blu-ray disks are types of optical storage media used to store and playback audio, video, and store data. These disks are read using a laser diode in a CD, DVD, or Blu-ray drive.

CDs typically holds about 700 MB of data or 80 minutes of audio. These disks were primarily used for storing music, but were also used for storing software, files, and game media. Somewhat obsolete nowadays.

DVDs commonly hold 4.7 GB (single layer) to 8.5 GB (dual layer). These disks were widely used for storing video (especially movies), as well as computer software, games, and file storage. Also relatively obsolete.

Standard single-layer Blu-ray disks hold up to 25 GB, and dual-layer discs can hold 50 GB. There are also multi-layer versions which can store up to 128 GB. These disks are primarily used to store high-definition movies (1080p and 4K), as well as large amounts of data and high-capacity software applications.

The data is stored as a spiral track starting from the centre of the disk. The track consists of a series of pits and lands. When the laser hits a pit, it reflects less light compared to when it hits a land, which reflects more light. Here we can see the pits and lands burned into the surface of the disk.

Here we've removed the metal casing so you can see the components inside.

A stepper motor moves the laser head assembly back and forth to the correct position on the disk, while the spindle motor rotates the disk at a constant speed.

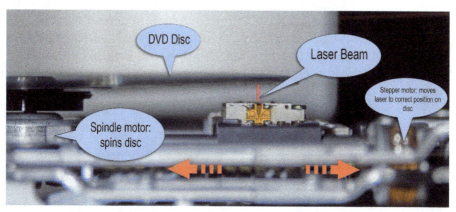

Here you can see a low powered laser beam focused onto the surface of the disk.

Lets take a closer look inside the laser head assembly. Here, we've broken the device down into its components.

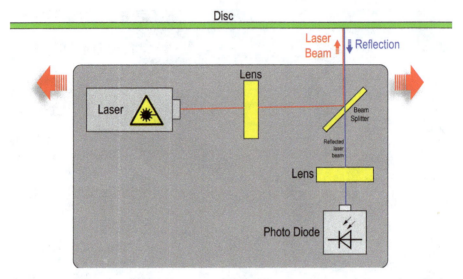

The green line across the top of the diagram represents the disk. This spins around when the drive is in use.

The grey box contains the laser and photo diodes used to read the pits in the surface of the disk.

The laser fires a beam of light that is focused through a lens onto the surface of the disk.

Now the pits and lands don't convert directly to 0s and 1s, this would be very inefficient. Instead, a change from pit to land or from land to pit corresponds to a binary 1, whereas no change corresponds to a binary 0. In the image below, I've magnified a track on a CD where you can see the pits and lands. I've marked out how the data is encoded.

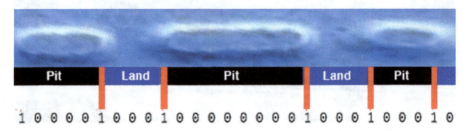

The number of zeroes between pit edges is determined by a specific encoding scheme (EFM in CDs, and EFM+ in DVDs).

Writeable Optical Disks

Writeable optical disks are a type of storage media that allows users to record data onto a disk using optical technology.

Writeable optical disks, such as CDs, DVDs and Blu-ray disks, come in two main formats: +R and -R (Dash R).

The "R" stands for "recordable" and the data can only be written once. Once data is written onto these disk, it cannot be altered or erased.

-R was introduced by Pioneer in 1997. It was one of the first writeable DVD formats to hit the market and gained significant popularity due to its compatibility with existing DVD players and drives. It was supported by various companies including Pioneer, Toshiba, Hitachi, and Panasonic. +R was developed a few years later, in 2002, by Philips and Sony. This format offered some technical advantages over-R, including faster writing speeds and more robust error management. +R was supported by a consortium of companies including Sony, Philips, Hewlett-Packard, Ricoh, and Yamaha.

You'll also find re-writeable disks labelled as RW. The "RW" label stands for "re-writeable", meaning data can be written, erased, and rewritten multiple times.

Most modern writeable drives support multiple formats, including -R/RW, +R/RW for CD, DVD and Blu-ray disks.

This provides users with flexibility in choosing the type of disks they need.

Memory Cards

Many laptops and tablets now have memory card readers built in. The most common memory card is the SD Card. This can be a full sized SD card or a Micro SD card.

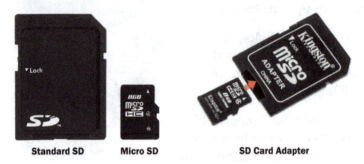

Standard SD   Micro SD   SD Card Adapter

Standard SD cards are commonly used in digital cameras, and many laptops have standard size SD card readers built in. Tablets, phones, and small cameras usually use micro SD cards.

You can get an SD Card adapter if your SD card reader does not read Micro SD cards.

There are various types of SD cards available, each marked with a speed classification symbol indicating the data transfer speed. If you are merely storing files, the data transfer speed doesn't matter as much. However, if you are using the card in a dash cam or digital camera, faster data transfer speeds are necessary. To be safe, the higher the speed, the better. You can see a summary in the table below.

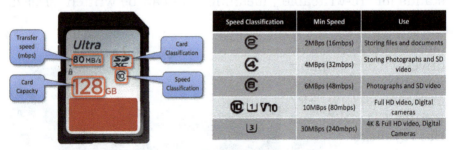

Speed Classification	Min Speed	Use
Ⓒ	2MBps (16mbps)	Storing files and documents
Ⓒ4	4MBps (32mbps)	Storing Photographs and SD video
Ⓒ6	6MBps (48mbps)	Photographs and SD video
Ⓒ10 U1 V10	10MBps (80mbps)	Full HD video, Digital cameras
U3	30MBps (240mbps)	4K & Full HD video, Digital Cameras

SDHC stands for "Secure Digital High Capacity", and supports capacities up to 32 GB.

SDXC stands for "Secure Digital eXtended Capacity", and supports capacities up to 2 TB.

SDUC stands for "Secure Digital Ultra Capacity", and supports capacities up to 128 TB.

These cards are usually read with a card reader. Most tablets and smart phones have these built in, however you can buy USB card readers that plug into your computer like the one below.

Most modern laptops or tablets have a built in reader. It is usually on either of the side panels or the front panel.

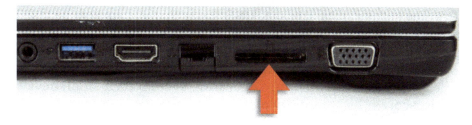

The card will show up as another drive in file explorer in Windows. Click on the drive to see the contents of the card.

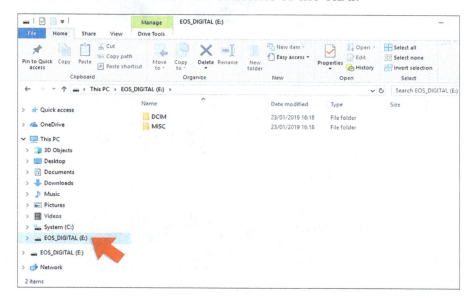

USB Flash Drives

USB flash drives, also known as memory sticks or thumb drives, are portable storage devices that connect to a computer's USB port. They use flash memory, a type of non-volatile memory that retains data without needing a power source. This makes them reliable for storing data over time. The drives come in a range of storage capacities, from as little as 2GB to over 512GB, catering to various data storage needs.

Typically, USB flash drives are formatted using FAT32 or exFAT file systems, ensuring compatibility with a wide range of operating systems, including Windows, macOS, and Linux. This allows them to be used across different devices without requiring reformatting, making data transfer between systems straightforward.

Beyond simple data storage, USB flash drives can also be used as bootable devices. This feature allows users to install or run operating systems directly from the flash drive, which is particularly useful for troubleshooting and recovery purposes. The ability to carry an entire operating system on a small device underscores the versatility of flash drives.

In terms of physical design, USB flash drives vary widely. They come in numerous shapes and sizes, often including protective casings or retractable connectors to safeguard the USB interface.

Despite their small size, they can store vast amounts of data, including documents, photos, videos, and software applications, making them a practical tool for both personal and professional use.

External Hard Disk

External hard disk drives (HDDs) are storage devices that are connected to a computer via a USB port, typically USB 2.0, USB 3.0, or USB-C. These drives are designed for portability and offer the convenience of external storage.

With their compact size, external HDDs are easily transportable, fitting comfortably in a pocket or bag. They serve as a reliable solution for data backup, allowing users to safeguard important files such as photos, documents, videos, and so on.

External HDDs are available in various storage capacities, ranging from smaller sizes to larger options exceeding 4TB and beyond. This wide range of capacities ensures users can choose the appropriate size to accommodate their storage needs.

The choice of file system depends on the intended use of the drive and the operating systems it will be connected to. If you want to use the drive on multiple different computers and platforms use exFAT. If it's windows only use NTFS. If it's a Mac only use HFS or AFS.

The versatility and convenience of external HDDs make them valuable tools for individuals and businesses, providing secure and portable storage options for reliable data management.

NAS Drives

NAS drives, sometimes called Network Attached Storage, allow you to store and backup files to a central point on a network.

A NAS drive usually contains one or more individual hard disk drives that can be formatted as a single drive, or as a RAID.

The drives are encased in a box similar to the one shown on the right.

A NAS drive has its own operating system which is usually some Linux derivative. Folders are created and shared on the NAS so that all the machines on the network can access the files in these folders. Shared data can either be set to private for one particular machine or shared publicly for all machines to see.

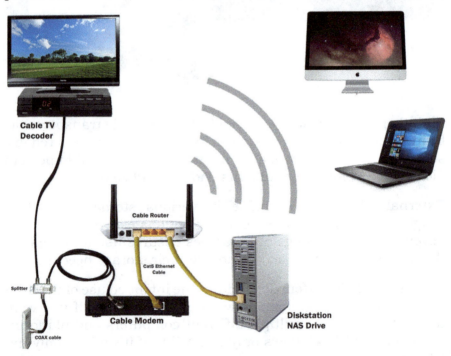

These devices make great backup strategies and come with software you can install on your computer to automate backups at certain times. You will need a few terabytes of storage on your NAS.

CPU / Processor

The CPU or processor is the brain of the computer and responds to all the commands you give the computer. It is one of the primary factors in determining the power of the system. Measured in Gigahertz, the higher the number, the more powerful the processor.

Modern processors have multiple cores. You might see a dual core or quad core processor. A core is an independent processing unit, meaning the processor can execute more than one instruction at a time, so the more cores your processor has, theoretically the faster it is.

The job of the CPU, is to execute a sequence of stored instructions called a program. The instructions are kept in the computer's memory (or RAM).

There are four steps that nearly all CPUs use in their operation:

Fetch, decode, execute, write-back

See "Fetch Execute Cycle" on page 183.

Inside the CPU

The CPU die shot marked in the diagram below is a simplified conceptual visual aid rather than a formal physical schematic, yet it shows the relationship between the internal components.

At the top you can see the clock. In the diagram it is illustrated as a single block for simplicity. The clock provides a repeating timing reference for the processor and is usually measured in gigahertz (GHz). This signal synchronizes the internal circuits so that every stage of the CPU operates in an ordered sequence at the defined frequency.

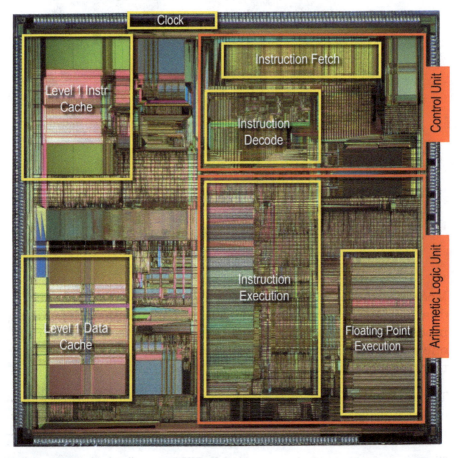

The Control Unit coordinates the execution of instructions and generates control signals that direct the operation of other components in the CPU, including the ALU, registers, cache system, and the external buses.

The instruction fetch circuit reads the next machine-code instruction bytes required from the instruction cache and places them into prefetch buffers (if it's not in the instruction cache, it is retrieved from main memory).

The machine-code bytes represent instructions, and are shown in hexadecimal form for human readability where each pair of hex digits represents one byte.

For example the machine-code bytes **B8 04 00 00 00** could represent the instruction **MOV EAX, 4**.

Here, **B8** is the opcode and it means move a 32-bit immediate value into the EAX register, and **04 00 00 00** is the 32-bit immediate operand equal to the integer value 4 in little-endian byte order.

The Arithmetic Logic Unit performs arithmetic, logic, and comparison operations on processor operands.

The instruction execution circuit carries out the operations specified by the decoded machine-code instruction. Integer operands supplied by registers or by the Level 1 data cache are routed through parallel adders, comparators, and logic gates to produce a result, which is written back to the registers. Whenever an execution operation affects program status, the ALU updates condition flags such as zero, sign, carry, or overflow so subsequent instructions can make decisions based on those outcomes.

The floating-point execution circuit performs mathematical operations on numbers represented in IEEE floating-point format when an instruction requires non-integer representations. Specialized arrays implement multiplication, division, and arithmetic on fractional values using hardware that is separate from the integer adders. Results from floating-point operations are returned to registers.

Level 1 instruction cache stores recently fetched machine-code instruction bytes in ultra-fast on-die memory so that the instruction circuitry can obtain the next opcodes without waiting for slower main memory.

Level 1 data cache stores recently used data values so operands can be delivered immediately to the ALU and floating-point execution circuitry without waiting for slower main memory.

Other Internal Components

Computers also contain other components that perform different tasks. Two common ones are a sound card and a video card. Other internal components include ethernet and WiFi cards for network connectivity.

Sound Card

A sound card, also known as an audio card, is an internal expansion card that facilitates the input and output of audio signals to and from a computer. This allows multimedia applications such as music, video, audio presentations, and games to play sound through a speaker or sound system.

There are several types of sound card such as integrated, dedicated and external. Integrated sound cards are built directly into the motherboard of most modern computers and provide sufficient audio quality for general tasks such as listening to music, watching videos, and casual gaming.

Dedicated sound cards, also known as plug-in cards, are installed in a PCIe slot on the motherboard. These cards use higher quality components, which result in superior audio clarity, better signal processing, and additional features. Dedicated sound cards are ideal for high-end applications like professional audio production, music composition, and video editing. They are preferred by users who require the best audio performance and advanced functionalities.

You might also find external audio interfaces that plug into the computer using USB.

These devices are particularly useful in professional audio production, live performances, and gaming.

Video Card

The video card or graphics card is responsible for processing video, graphic, and visual effects you see on your monitor.

The market is primarily dominated by two main manufacturers, NVIDIA and AMD, who continuously push the envelope by advancing their technologies with features like ray tracing and AI enhancements.

The heart of the video card, the GPU (Graphics Processing Unit), is tasked with processing data and executing instructions to render graphics.

Video cards are categorized into two types: integrated and dedicated. Integrated video cards are typically embedded within the CPU itself or mounted on the motherboard allowing it to sharing resources such as memory with the CPU. These are suitable for everyday tasks such as web browsing, office applications, and video streaming, but they may struggle with more graphics-intensive applications like modern video games or professional-grade video editing and 3D rendering.

Dedicated video cards are separate units that plug into a PCIe slot on the motherboard. These cards come with their own specialized memory, known as VRAM, which is used to store graphical data. This high speed memory is crucial for efficiently processing high-resolution textures, graphics and complex 3D environments.

Dedicated video cards are suitable for handling graphically intensive tasks, such as high-end gaming, professional video editing, and intricate 3D rendering

The type of video card depends on computing requirements and the performance demands of the applications being used.

Network Cards

A Network Card, also known as a Network Interface Card (NIC) is a hardware component that allows a computer to connect to a network, facilitating communication with other computes and devices as well as access to the internet.

NICs can be integrated onto the motherboard or added as separate expansion cards (PCIe or M2), and they come in various forms, including wired (Ethernet) and wireless (Wi-Fi).

Wired NICs use Ethernet cables for reliable and high-speed data transmission, supporting speeds from 10 Mbps to 10 Gbps and beyond. Common standards for

these NICs include Fast Ethernet, Gigabit Ethernet, and 10 Gigabit Ethernet, with connections typically made via RJ-45 ports. Wired NICs are particularly useful in desktops, servers, and network infrastructure where stable and fast connections are crucial.

Wireless NICs provide the flexibility of connecting to Wi-Fi networks, eliminating the need for physical cables. These NICs adhere to Wi-Fi standards such as IEEE 802.11a/b/g/n/ac/ax, with the latest currently Wi-Fi 6 (802.11ax), which offers faster speeds and improved performance in dense environments.

M.2 cards are small and designed to fit into the M.2 slot on the motherboard (as shown above). They are commonly used in modern laptops and some desktops. USB wireless NICs plug into any available USB port on the laptop or desktop and often require minimal setup.

Capture Cards

Capture cards are specialized hardware devices used to capture and record video and audio signals from various external sources, such as cameras, gaming consoles, and other multimedia devices. They are essential tools for content creators, gamers, and professionals who need to record, stream, or broadcast high-quality video content.

The most common interface for modern capture cards is HDMI. An HDMI cable plugs into the capture card and the card itself often plugs into a USB port. Although there are also internal capture cards that plug into a PCIe slot on the motherboard.

In the example below, I have a camera connected to the capture card that is plugged into a USB port on my laptop. A free software application called OBS Studio is being used to record the footage from the camera.

Many capture cards feature real-time encoding, with built-in hardware encoders that reduce the load on the computer's CPU to ensure smooth recording or streaming.

Expansion Slots

PCI Express (PCIe) slots are the standard expansion slots used in modern motherboards. They provide high-speed connections for various expansion cards such as graphics cards, sound cards, network cards, and SSDs. Here in the photograph below, we can see the PCIe slots on the motherboard.

PCIe slots come in different sizes, each suited to different types of devices and performance requirements.

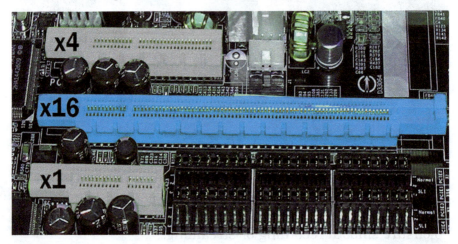

PCIe x1 slot has a single lane and is the smallest PCIe slot. It is used for low-bandwidth devices such as sound cards, network interface cards (NICs), USB expansion cards, and low-power SSDs.

PCIe x4 slot has four lanes and offers more bandwidth than the PCIe x1 slot. It is commonly used for NVMe SSDs and RAID controllers.

PCIe x8 slot has eight lanes and provides even more bandwidth, suitable for high-speed network cards and some lower-end graphics cards.

PCIe x16 slot has sixteen lanes and is the largest and fastest standard PCIe slot to date. It is primarily used for high-end graphics cards that require substantial bandwidth for data transfer.

This is known as the Link width, which is the number of simultaneous lanes used in a PCIe connection. Each lane consists of two pairs of wires: one pair for transmitting data and the other for receiving data.

The bandwidth of PCIe slots depends on the version or generation and the number of lanes they support. Bandwidth refers to the maximum rate at which data can be transferred in a given amount of time, usually measured in gigabytes per second (GB/s).

Each new generation of PCIe improves upon the previous one by increasing the data transfer rates and overall performance. The table below shows a summary.

Link Width	PCIe Gen-1	PCIe Gen-2	PCIe Gen-3	PCIe Gen-4
x1	250 MB/s	500 MB/s	1 GB/s	2 GB/s
x4	1 GB/s	2 GB/s	4 GB/s	8 GB/s
x8	2 GB/s	4 GB/s	8 GB/s	16 GB/s
x16	4 GB/s	8 GB/s	16 GB/s	32 GB/s

Also newer generations are backward compatible with the previous ones.

For example, you can use a PCIe Gen-3 card in a PCIe Gen-4 slot, but it will operate at the PCIe Gen-3 speed.

The Motherboard

All the components connect to a large circuit board called a motherboard, which is the main circuit board found in desktop and laptop computer systems. It hosts many crucial components, such as the processor (or CPU) and memory (or RAM), and provides connectors for other peripherals.

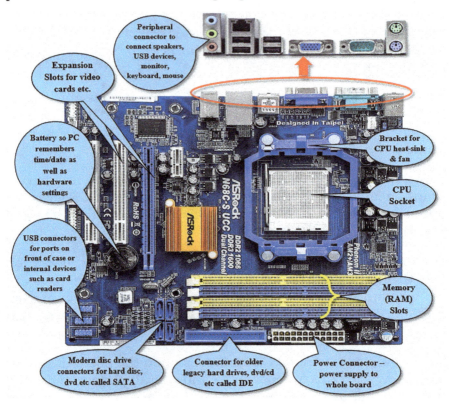

In a typical desktop computer, the CPU, main memory (RAM), and other essential components are connected to this board. Other components such as storage devices (hard disks, DVD drives) are linked via cables to drive connectors on the motherboard (typically SATA). Video display and sound cards may be integrated directly into the motherboard or plugged into expansion slots. In modern computers, it is increasingly common for some peripherals, specifically video and sound cards, to be integrated directly onto the motherboard.

On the back panel, you'll find numerous ports for Video, USB, Ethernet, and Audio.

Form Factor

The form factor is the standardized shape and layout of the motherboard. Most motherboards sold today are either Mini-ITX, Micro-ATX or Standard-ATX.

Standard ATX
305 x 244 mm

Micro ATX
244 x 244 mm

Mini ITX
170 x 170 mm

Nano ITX
120 x 120 mm

Pico ITX
72 x 10 mm

The most common motherboard form factor is ATX. ATX is short for Advanced Technology Extended and is a specification used to outline motherboard and power supply configurations.

Introduced in 1995, the ATX motherboard specification included IO support, and placed all the required connectors for keyboard/mouse as well as other external peripherals directly on the motherboard.

Trusted Platform Module

The Trusted Platform Module (or TPM) is a chip usually mounted on the motherboard that securely stores passwords, certificates, or encryption keys that are used to authenticate a PC or laptop so that malware can't access or tamper with that data

Discrete TPMs are dedicated chips that implement TPM functionality in their own tamper resistant semiconductor package. Integrated TPMs are part of another chip. Firmware TPMs (fTPMs) are firmware-based solutions that run in a CPU's trusted execution environment. Intel, AMD and Qualcomm have implemented firmware TPMs.

The Chipset

A chipset is the circuit that orchestrates the flow of data to and from key components of the motherboard, such as CPU to memory, as well as the data flow to and from hard drives, external drives, and peripherals.

North Bridge, South Bridge & PCH

The north bridge was used to connect the CPU to the RAM and the PCI Express Lane.

The south bridge connected the CPU to the slower devices such as USB ports, hard drives, external drives, printers wifi/network cards, and other peripherals.

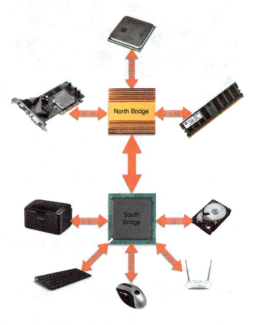

In modern computer architectures, the traditional North and South Bridge components have been largely integrated into the CPU and the Platform Controller Hub (PCH).

The PCH consolidates the functions of the South Bridge and some functions of the North Bridge. While the primary PCIe lanes (eg high end graphics cards) are controlled by the CPU, the PCH also handles additional PCIe lanes used for connecting slower peripherals.

DMI (Direct Media Interface) serves as the primary data pathway between the CPU and the PCH, allowing the CPU to communicate with other components such as storage devices, USB ports, network & audio cards.

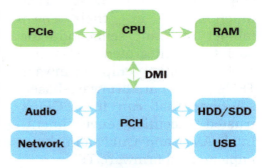

CPU Socket

This is a master socket mounted on the motherboard for housing the CPU. These sockets are known as Zero Insertion Force (or ZIF) meaning the CPU drops into the socket and secured with a locking lever. This allows the CPU to be replaced or upgraded.

There are various types of socket. For example, the Intel Core i5 uses Socket LGA 1156, Core 2 Duo uses socket LGA 775, and the AMD Ryzen 5 uses Socket AM4. Each CPU type is only compatible with its own socket type.

The microchip itself is packaged inside a durable plastic, metal, or ceramic casing which protects the chip and allows for better cooling. A heatsink fits over the top of the CPU to remove heat.

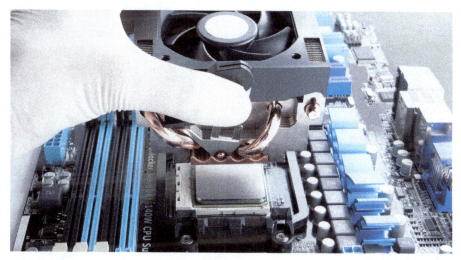

The BIOS

The BIOS (Basic Input/Output System) is a fundamental firmware component integral to the functioning of a computer system and is stored in a small memory chip located on the motherboard. This chip is typically a form of non-volatile memory, such as ROM (Read-Only Memory), EEPROM (Electrically Erasable  Programmable Read-Only Memory), or flash memory, which allows it to retain data even when the computer is powered off.

When the computer is powered on, the BIOS conducts a Power On Self Test (POST) to verify that essential hardware components like the CPU, RAM, and storage devices are functioning correctly.

Once the POST completes successfully, the BIOS firmware initiates the Bootstrap Loader, also known as the bootloader. The bootloader's primary function is to locate and load the operating system's kernel or boot image from the hard drive into memory.

Beyond these initial startup functions, the BIOS also provides an interface for configuring hardware settings.

```
                         BIOS SETUP UTILITY
 Main    OC Tweaker    Advanced    H/W Monitor    Boot    Security    Exit

 System Overview                               Use [ENTER], [TAB]
                                               or [SHIFT-TAB] to
 System Time             [20:37:35]            select a field.
 System Date             [Tue 05/14/2019]
                                               Use [+] or [-] to
 BIOS Version      : N68C-S UCC P1.60          configure system Time.
 Processor Type    : AMD Phenom(tm) II X6 1045T
                     Processor (64bit)
 Processor Speed   : 2712MHz
 Microcode Update  : 100FA0/10000BF
 L1 Cache Size     : 768KB
 L2 Cache Size     : 3072KB
 L3 Cache Size     : 6144KB                    ↔     Select Screen
                                               ↑↓    Select Item
 Total Memory      : 8192MB                    +-    Change Field
                     Dual-Channel Memory Mode  Tab   Select Field
```

While traditional BIOS firmware may still be found in some older systems or legacy environments, its use is largely obsolete as UEFI has become the prevalent firmware standard in modern computing.

UEFI

Commonly pronounced "yoofey", or "yoo-ee-fey", the acronym stands for Unified Extensible Firmware Interface and replaces the old BIOS in modern PCs.

Like the BIOS, UEFI checks what hardware components are connected at boot, and performs various start up tests (POST).

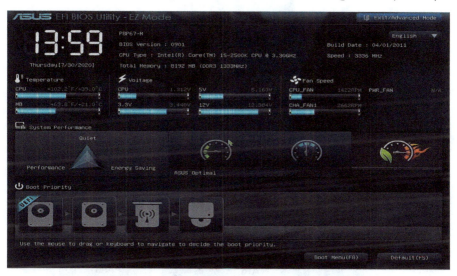

UEFI scans the GPTs (or partition tables) of the attached hard disk drives to find an EFI Service/System Partition - a partition that stores the EFI bootloader. The boot loader then starts the operating system from the correct partition.

In the illustration below, you can see the EFI system partition and the partition containing the operating system on Disk 1.

UEFI is also programmable and can reside in a folder in flash memory on the motherboard, but can also be stored on a storage or network drive. This means manufacturers and developers can add applications and drivers, allowing UEFI to function as a lightweight operating system.

UEFI is more secure, providing features such as Secure Boot.

79

System on a Chip

A system on a chip (or SoC) is an integrated circuit that combines the components of a computer system into a single chip. These components usually include the CPU, RAM, Storage (eg SSD) and a GPU.

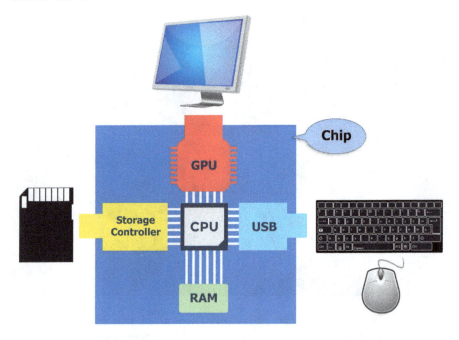

A recent example of a system on a chip is Apple's M1 chip used in the new line of Apple Mac computers.

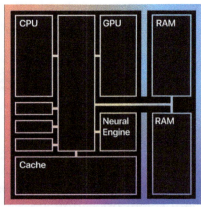

The M1 chip combines the CPU, Graphics Processor (or GPU), memory (or RAM), SSD drive controller, and a neural engine which is a component designed to use machine learning and artificial intelligence for tasks such identifying objects in photos, or applying an automatic filter to a picture, analysing videos, voice recognition, and so on. The M1 also includes a thunderbolt controller with USB 4 support, and a few other minor components.

Power Supplies

The power supply (PSU) converts high voltage electricity from the mains power supply (usually 110-240v AC), into regulated low-voltage DC power for the internal components of a computer.

There have been many different types of power supply in the past, however the computer industry eventually settled on using the ATX power supply.

ATX stands for Advanced Technology eXtended and is a motherboard and power supply configuration specification developed by Intel in 1995.

For modern systems, most power supplies produce three primary voltages:

- 12 volts
- 5 volts
- 3.3 volts

Some power supplies also produce negative voltages of -5v, -12v together with a +5v standby voltage, although negative voltages are rarely used in modern systems.

The internal components of a computer require different voltages to operate.

+3.3v is used to power the Chipset, CPU, RAM DIMMs, PCIe

+5v is used to power the on board disk drive logic, and low-voltage motors in 2.5" hard disk drives, and USB devices.

+12v is used to power drive motors in 3.5" hard disk drives and DVD drives, as well as high end PCIe graphics cards.

On this particular power supply, you'll see the power outputs on the specs printed on the side of the case.

MODEL (型号) : OCZ600MXSP						
AC INPUT(輸入): 100-240V 10A	DC OUTPUT (直流电输出)					
	+5V	+3.3V	+12V₁	+12V₂	-12V	+5VSB
FREQUENCY (频率) : 50-60Hz	25A	25A	25A	25A	0.3A	2.5A
MAX. LOAD (最大载): 600W	150W		504W		3.6W	12.5W

The wattage is the maximum amount of power the power supply can output under a maximum load. So the 600W power supply shown here can distribute up to 600 watts to the computer's motherboard and various components.

The power supply distributes power to the various components using connectors.

A 24 pin molex connector plugs into a 24 pin power port on the motherboard. On some older motherboards, the detachable 4 pins on the end sometimes plug into a separate port next to the CPU.

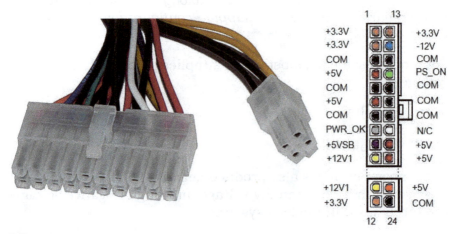

You'll also find various other plugs for disk internal drives. The older 4 pin molex connectors. The yellow wire carries 12v, the red wire carries 5v. Black is ground.

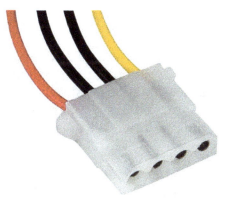

For newer disk drives, you'll find SATA power connectors. Yellow is 12v, red is 5v, blue/orange is 3.3v, black is ground.

Some PSUs will include some other connectors for high end graphics cards and motherboards that require additional power. These are usually 8, 6 or 4 pin molex connectors. Yellow is 12v.

Cooling Systems

Since dense electronics produces a lot of heat, cooling systems are essential components in maintaining the optimal operating temperature of computer hardware.

When components such as the CPU and GPU are under heavy load, they generate heat, which, if not dissipated efficiently, can lead to performance degradation, instability, or even permanent damage to the hardware. Cooling systems are designed to mitigate this heat buildup and maintain a safe operating temperature.

Air cooling is the most common and cost-effective cooling method used in computer systems. It relies on fans and heat sinks to dissipate heat. You'll often find large heat sinks and fans attached to CPUs and graphics cards (GPU) to remove the heat from the components. Heat sinks are metal structures with a large surface area that draw heat away from the component and dissipate it to the surrounding area.

You'll also sometimes find large case fans on desktop PCs that expel the heat from inside the system.

Liquid cooling, also known as water cooling, is a more advanced and efficient cooling method. It utilizes a closed-loop system to transfer heat away from the components.

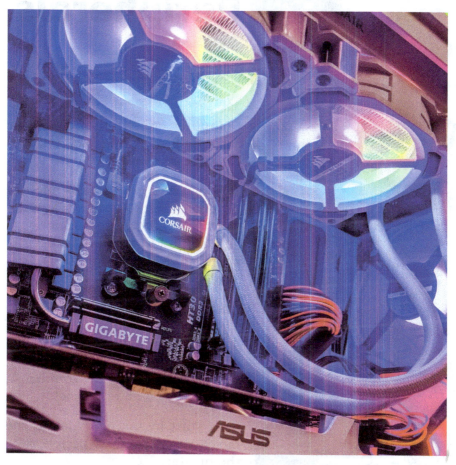

Water blocks are installed directly on the CPU, GPU, or other components. These water blocks are connected to large radiators mounted to the case. The coolant is pumped around the circuit, drawing heat away from the water blocks to the radiators. Large fans blow air across the radiator moving the heat outside.

Liquid cooling systems offer superior cooling efficiency than air coolers. By transferring heat through liquid coolant, they can dissipate more heat than air cooling. Liquid cooling is especially beneficial for highly overclocked or power-hungry processors and GPUs, as it provides better temperature management and stability under heavy loads.

3

Computer Peripherals

Computer peripherals are essentially anything that connects to the computer.

This can be input devices such as keyboards, mice and scanners; output devices such as monitors and printers; or storage devices such as hard disks, DVD and flash drives.

All these components connect to the computer using a variety of different connectors and cables; whether it's USB to connect a printer or HDMI to connect a computer screen or projector.

Let's start by taking a look at the most common of all peripherals, the printer.

Have a look at the video demos to help you understand. Open your web browser and navigate to the following website:

elluminetpress.com/hw-per

Printers

A printer is a peripheral device that makes a permanent representation of a graphic or text on paper known as a hard copy. Printers come in two main types: inkjet and laser.

Inkjet Printer

These printers are good for the average user who just wants to print some letters or other documents and the odd few photographs. They are generally slower printers and are not suitable for printing documents with a large number of pages.

These printers can also print on labels, envelopes and specialist presentation paper (good for greetings cards if you want to print your own).

The only issue I find with inkjet printers is the ink tends to dry up if you don't print out regularly. So make sure you print out something at least once a week to keep the ink from drying up.

Inkjet printers work by forcing out tiny droplets of ink in a pattern to form an image on the page. As you can see in the image below, the inkjet heads are on the bottom of the cartridge which is suspended above the paper.

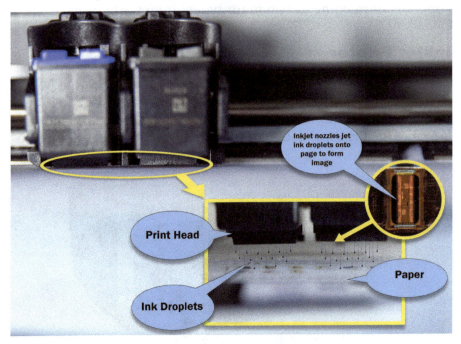

The printer precisely controls which nozzles release ink and when, based on the digital data it received.

In printers that use thermal technology, the nozzles have tiny heating element that heats up, causing the ink to vaporize and form a bubble. As the bubble expands, it forces a droplet of ink out of the nozzle onto the paper. The process happens rapidly, allowing for fast printing.

In printers that use piezoelectric technology, the nozzles have piezoelectric crystals. When a voltage is applied to these crystals, they change shape, forcing a droplet of ink out of the nozzle. This method allows for more precise control over the size and placement of ink droplets.

Here in the photo on the right, you can see a strip of nozzles for each primary color (Yellow, Magenta, Cyan).

Laser Printer

Laser printers produce high quality prints very quickly and are suited to high volumes of printouts. These printers are good if you do a lot of printing, for example, if you run a business or have a family that all want to print out from their own computers/laptops at the same time.

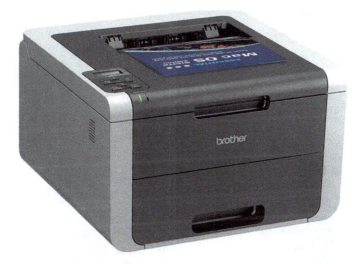

These printers can print in black and white or color and work by melting a fine powder (called toner) onto the page. The toner cartridges are expensive to buy but last a lot longer than ink jet cartridges. Here we have black, cyan, magenta and yellow.

Laser printers use a laser beam to create the image to be printed on an electro-statically charged rotating drum. A corona wire gives the drum a negative electrostatic charge of anywhere between a hundred and a few thousand volts. The laser creates the image to be printed by selectively discharging areas of the drum. These areas exposed by the laser have a reduced negative charge or are neutralized, while the unexposed areas retain their full negative charge.

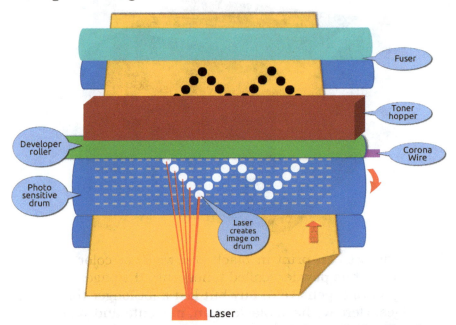

The toner which is also negatively charged, is applied to the drum and is attracted to the areas that the laser exposed (the less-charged or neutralized areas). The rest of the toner is repelled by the unexposed (still negatively charged) areas of the drum due to like charges repelling each other.

A sheet of paper (often given a positive charge) is then rolled under the drum, and the toner is transferred from the drum to the paper. The paper then passes through a fuser unit that melts the toner onto the paper.

The charge applied depends on the type of electro-photographic process used. There are two types: positive and negative. My laser printer works as described above as I've measured the charges on the drum, however on some printer models, the static charges are reversed, but the principle is the same.

Other Peripherals

Other peripherals include scanners, cameras, game control pads, virtual reality headsets, and so on.

Most external peripherals connect to the computer through a data port using a USB cable. Some older peripherals connect using firewire, but most use USB. eSATA ports can connect certain external hard drives. The SPDIF port is an optical audio port that allows you to connect high end sound systems.

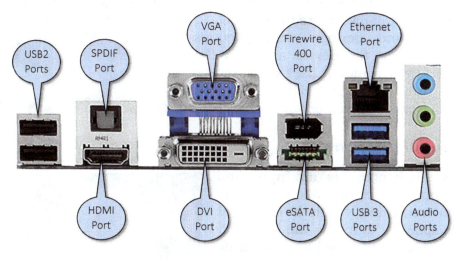

Monitors, projectors and other screens are connected using either HDMI, VGA or DVI.

3.5mm phono jacks are used to connect microphones and speaker systems to a computer.

- The blue port is called 'line in' and is used to connect external audio devices for recording.

- The green port is called 'line out' and is used to connect speaker systems and headphones.

- The pink port is called 'mic in' and is used to connect microphones.

Keyboards

A keyboard is a primary input device that allows users to input text, commands, and other data into a computer. It typically consists of an arrangement of buttons or keys, including letters, numbers, symbols, and special function keys. Keyboards can be wired or wireless, and they connect to the computer via USB, Bluetooth, or other interfaces.

Mouse

A mouse is a pointing device used to control the cursor on a computer screen. It allows users to select, click, drag, and perform other actions by moving the device across a flat surface. The mouse uses a light sensor to track movement. Like keyboards, mice can be wired or wireless.

Touchscreens

A touchscreen is an input and output device that allows users to interact directly with the computer display by touching the screen. It eliminates the need for a separate pointing device like a mouse. Touchscreens can be found on various devices, including smartphones, tablets, laptops, and all-in-one computers. They use different technologies, such as resistive, capacitive, or infrared, to detect touch input.

Monitors

A monitor, also known as a display or screen, is an output device that visually presents data or information generated by the computer.

It provides a visual interface for users to view text, images, videos, and graphical user interfaces (GUIs). Monitors come in different sizes, resolutions, and types (LCD, LED, OLED) and connect to the computer's graphics card or integrated graphics output using display port, HDMI, VGA or DVI.

Speakers

Speakers are output devices that produce sound or audio generated by the computer. They allow users to listen to music, videos, system sounds, and other audio content. Speakers can vary in size, power, and audio quality. They can be built into monitors, laptops, or other devices, or they can be external and connected to the computer's audio output ports.

Scanners

Scanners are input devices used to convert physical documents, images, or photos into digital format. They capture the image or text on the document and convert it into a digital file that can be stored, edited, or shared on a computer. Scanners can be  flatbed (where the document is placed on a glass surface) or sheet-fed (where the document is fed through the scanner).

Webcams

Webcams are small cameras designed to capture video for real-time communication or recording purposes. They are often used for video calls, online meetings, live streaming, or video recording. Webcams are typically connected to computers via USB and can be built into laptops, and some monitors. Webcams have become especially important in recent years with the  rise of remote work and online communication.

Data Ports

Data ports allow you to connect devices to your computer. The most common data ports are USB, Ethernet.

USB

Universal Serial Bus (USB) is an industry standard that specifies the requirements for cables, connectors, and protocols for connection, communication, and power supply between computers and peripheral devices. Developed in the mid-1990s, USB has become a cornerstone of modern computer hardware, facilitating the connection of a wide range of external devices.

USB supports plug-and-play, a feature that allows users to connect devices to a USB port and use them immediately without the need to reboot or install additional drivers. Moreover, each USB port delivers power in addition to data, simplifying the setup and use of peripheral devices.

In terms of connectors, the Type-A connector is the original rectangular design that is unidirectional, predominantly used on host devices like desktop computers.

Type-B connectors are generally found on larger peripheral devices such as printers and external hard drives.

USB 2 Type B   **USB 3 Type B**

Mini and Micro USB connectors, which are smaller, were commonly used for mobile devices and digital cameras. However, Micro USB remains prevalent in many devices today, although it is increasingly being replaced by the more versatile USB Type-C connector.

USB 2 Mini   **USB 2 Micro**   **USB 3 Micro**

The evolution of USB has been marked by a series of iterations or versions, each introducing significant improvements in data transfer speeds, power capabilities, and overall efficiency.

USB 1.x released in 1996, featured a data rate of 1.5 Mbps for simple peripheral connections, and up to 12 Mbps for higher-performance devices such as scanners, and early storage devices. Revised in 1998 as USB 1.1 to improve reliability and interoperability, while retaining the same speed classes.

USB 2.0 was introduced in 2000, and significantly increased the data transfer rate to 480 Mbps.

The USB 3.x series often color coded blue and marked with the SS (SuperSpeed) logo, brought an even faster data transfer rate. USB 3.0, which launched in 2008 and later rebranded as USB 3.1 Gen 1, offered speeds up to 5 Gbps. It introduced a dual-bus architecture to maintain backward compatibility with USB 2.0 devices.

USB 3.1, or USB 3.1 Gen 2, followed in 2013, doubling the data transfer rate to 10 Gbps and improving power delivery.

In 2017, USB 3.2 was announced, which can reach up to 20 Gbps through a multi-lane operation.

USB C

USB-C is a 24-pin USB connector system favored for its enhanced design and functionality compared to older USB types. These connectors feature a reversible design, meaning there is no wrong way to plug them in, which eliminates the common frustration associated with the non-reversible Type A connectors.

USB-C supports different data transfer speeds depending on the USB version it's using. Initially with USB 3.1, it supported speeds up to 10 Gbps. Later standards have enhanced these capabilities. USB 3.2 increases speeds to 20 Gbps, and USB4 boosts them to 40 Gbps. USB-C can also transmit high-definition video and audio, with support for resolutions up to 4K and beyond. Additionally, when used with compatible devices that support Thunderbolt 3 or 4, USB-C can enhance data transfer rates even further and connect high-resolution displays through just one cable.

USB-C can deliver up to 100 watts of power, enabling it to charge mobile devices like smartphones and tablets as well as power larger devices. As a result, many new tablets and phones now come equipped with USB-C ports.

Similarly, an increasing number of modern laptops are incorporating USB-C ports due to their versatility and power delivery capabilities.

Ethernet

Ethernet is a widely adopted family of networking technologies primarily used for local area networks (LANs). At home, you typically use Cat5e or Cat6 cables to connect devices such as computers, gaming consoles, and smart TVs to your router to provide internet access.

The standard Ethernet plug used for twisted pair cables is the RJ-45 connector as shown below.

FireWire

Also known as IEEE 1394 or iLink, the FireWire port was widely used in digital camcorders. Most camcorders that recorded onto tape included a FireWire interface.

There were two versions: FireWire 400 (on the left) and FireWire 800 (on the right).

FireWire 400 transfers data at about 400 Mbps, while FireWire 800 transfers data at about 800 Mbps

ThunderBolt

Thunderbolt ports are high-speed data transfer interfaces that can support transfer speeds of up to 40Gbps, depending on the version. Thunderbolt 1 & 2 used the mini display connector and is somewhat slow & obsolete. Thunderbolt 3 & 4 uses the USB-C connector and has a data transfer speed of up to 40Gbps.

Thunderbolt 1 & 2   Thunderbolt 3 & 4

Thunderbolt ports are standard on many Macs and used for connecting peripherals, external displays, and high-speed data storage. A Thunderbolt 3/4 device can be plugged into a USB-C port, but it will only work to the extent that the USB-C port's capabilities allow.

eSATA

eSATA cables connect to some types of high speed external portable hard drives. The eSATA cable cannot transmit power, unless you use eSATAp (powered eSATA).

Video Ports

Monitors/computer screens and projectors connect to your PC or laptop using a variety of different connectors.

Many tablets and smaller computers have micro versions of these ports, eg micro USB or micro HDMI

DVI

Digital Video Interface is a video display interface used to connect a video source (eg your computer) to a display device, such as an HD ready TV, computer monitor or projector. You can get standard DVI, Mini DVI and Micro DVI.

DVI can get a bit confusing, as there are a number of different connectors. Here is a summary.

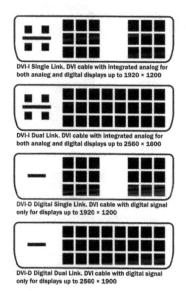

DVI-I Single Link. DVI cable with integrated analog for both analog and digital displays up to 1920 × 1200

DVI-I Dual Link. DVI cable with integrated analog for both analog and digital displays up to 2560 × 1600

DVI-D Digital Single Link. DVI cable with digital signal only for displays up to 1920 × 1200

DVI-D Digital Dual Link. DVI cable with digital signal only for displays up to 2560 × 1900

HDMI

High Definition Media Interface, is a combined audio/video interface for carrying video and audio data from a High Definition device such as a games console or computer to a high end computer monitor, video projector, or High Definition digital television.

Pictured below is Standard HDMI for TVs and DVD players, HDMI Mini for cameras, and Micro HDMI for small cameras, tablets and smartphones.

HDMI (High-Definition Multimedia Interface) has undergone several updates since its original release, with each version bringing new features, improved performance, and enhanced capabilities.

HDMI Version	Release Date	Bandwidth	Key Features
1.0	Dec 2002	4.95 Gbps	Supports 1080p at 60 Hz, 8 audio channels, 192 kHz/24-bit audio. Basic standard for HD content.
1.1	May 2004	4.95 Gbps	Added support for DVD Audio, allowing high-quality audio playback from DVDs.
1.2	Aug 2005	4.95 Gbps	Added support for One Bit Audio from Super Audio CDs, enhancing audio clarity and detail.
1.3	June 2006	10.2 Gbps	Supports Dolby TrueHD and DTS-HD for lossless audio, increased color depth (Deep Color).
1.4	June 2009	10.2 Gbps	Introduced Ethernet Channel, Audio Return Channel (ARC), 3D over HDMI, and 4K resolution at 30 Hz.
2.0	Sept 2013	18 Gbps	Enhanced support for 4K at 60 Hz, up to 32 audio channels for immersive audio, improved audio synchronization.
2.1	Nov 2017	48 Gbps	Enables 8K at 60 Hz and 4K at 120 Hz, supports Dynamic HDR, eARC for advanced audio formats over ARC.

VGA

Video Graphics Array is a 15-pin connector found on many computers and laptops and is used to connect to projectors, computer monitors and LCD television sets.

Component Video

Carries a video signal (no audio) that has been split into three component channels: red, green, blue. It is often used to connect high end DVD players to televisions.

Composite Video

Carries an analogue standard definition video signal combining red, green, blue channels (with no audio) and is used in old games consoles or analogue video cameras.

Audio Ports

1/8" (3.5mm) Phono

The phono jack also known as an audio jack, headphone jack or jack plug, is commonly used to connect speakers or headphones to a computer, laptop, tablet or MP3 player and carries analogue audio signals.

1/4" (6.35mm) Phono

These are generally used on a wide range of professional audio equipment. 6.35 mm (1/4 inch) plugs are common on audio recorders, musical instruments such as guitars and amps. These come in stereo and mono.

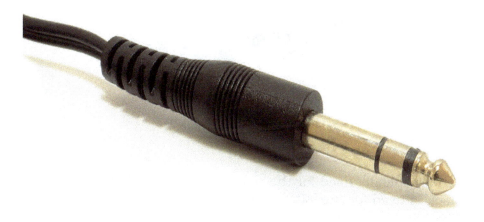

3 Pin XLR

The XLR connector is usually found on professional audio, video, and stage lighting equipment.

Many audio mixing desks have XLR connectors to connect stage mics and instruments.

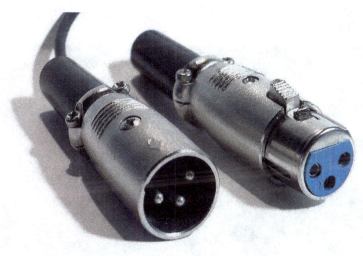

RCA Audio

RCA connectors are cylindrical plugs with a central pin and an outer metal ring or "shield." The central pin carries the audio signal, while the outer ring serves as a ground connection. They're designed for easy insertion and removal.

Red is typically used for the right audio channel, while white or black is used for the left audio channel.

RCA audio cables and connectors are still commonly used today for connecting analog audio devices such as CD players and turntables to amplifiers or receivers.

SPDIF

SPDIF stands for Sony/Philips Digital Interchange Format and is an interface standard used to connect consumer audio equipment.

It supports two primary connection methods: coaxial and optical. The coaxial connection uses a coaxial cable with an orange RCA connector.

The optical connection uses an optical cable with TOSLINK connectors and are immune to electromagnetic interference.

SPDIF is commonly used in home theater setups to transmit digital audio signals from TVs, media players, and streaming devices to AV receivers or soundbars. This enables immersive surround sound playback for movies, TV shows, and other multimedia content.

One of the advantages of the SPDIF interface is that it provides high-quality, noise-free signal transmission, which is important for digital audio.

Another advantage is that it allows for the transmission of compressed audio streams such as Dolby Digital (AC-3) and DTS (Digital Theater Systems), which can provide high-quality audio with lower data rates than uncompressed audio.

4

Computer Networks

When two or more computers are connected together they are said to be networked. A network can be two or three computers connected together in a small office or connect computers together in different parts of the country.

There are three main types of networks. LAN, MAN & WAN.

You can have either a client server or a peer to peer network model, depending on the environment in which the network is being used.

Networks can be set up using various topologies, such as star, bus, or ring networks.

Machines on the network can be linked together using Cat5, 6, or 7 ethernet cable, fibre optic cable, and cellular or WiFi.

Have a look at the video demos to help you understand. Open your web browser and navigate to the following website:

elluminetpress.com/net

Local Area Networks (LANs)

A small network contained in a single site or building is called a LAN or Local Area Network.

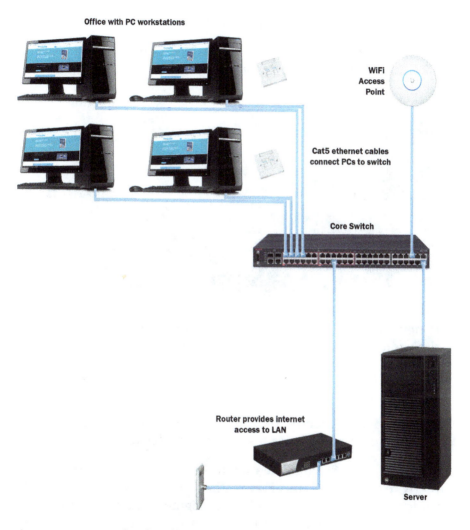

Office with PC workstations

WiFi Access Point

Cat5 ethernet cables connect PCs to switch

Core Switch

Router provides internet access to LAN

Server

As you can see in the diagram, the network covers a small area. The computers could be split up into different offices or all in one room and can all access resources served from the file server and use internet services provided by the router.

The machines are connected to a switch using Cat 5 cable. Some devices such as laptops, tablets and phones can be connected wirelessly through a WiFi access point.

Virtual LAN (VLAN)

A virtual local area network (VLAN) is a logical network segment created within a physical network infrastructure. It enables the partitioning of a single network into multiple isolated virtual networks, regardless of the physical connectivity of devices.

All network devices, including computers, printers, and servers, are connected to the same physical network switches.

The network administrator assigns specific ports on the network switch to each VLAN. For example on the switch above

VLAN01 is on ports 1 - 8
VLAN02 is on ports 9 - 16

So any device connected to ports 1 - 8 are on VLAN01, and any devices connected to ports 9 - 16 are on VLAN02.

By default, VLANs are isolated from one another and cannot directly exchange data. Each VLAN operates as a separate broadcast domain, creating a logical segmentation within a much larger network. However, if there is a need for communication between VLANs, it can be achieved through inter-VLAN routing. Some switches have built-in Layer 3 routing capabilities. These switches have VLAN interfaces, often referred to as Switched Virtual Interfaces (SVIs), associated with each VLAN. Each SVI acts as a virtual interface representing a specific VLAN. The Layer 3 switch performs the inter-VLAN routing internally, allowing devices in different VLANs to communicate.

Metropolitan Area Networks (MANs)

A metropolitan area network is a network that connects computers in a region larger than a local area network (LAN) but smaller than a wide area network (WAN), and is usually an interconnection of networks in a city that form a single larger network.

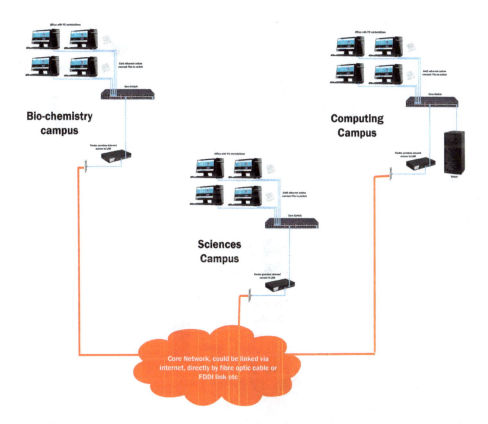

In this example, we have a university campus network with buildings spread all over the city. Each campus has its own LAN, and the LAN at each campus is linked together to form a much larger network called a MAN.

MANs are typically connected using a combination of wired and wireless technologies. This could be fiber optic cabling, leased lines, or virtual private networks (VPN) over public networks such as the internet.

MANs offer longer-distance coverage compared to LANs.

Wide Area Networks (WANs)

A network that connects computers and LANs together in different parts of the country or world is called a WAN or Wide Area Network.

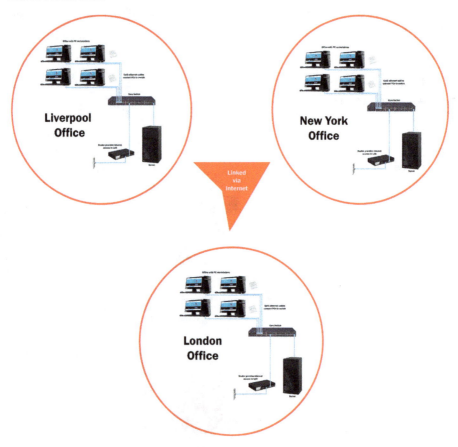

This example is of a multinational organisation that has offices in different cities and countries. Each organisation can have its own LAN and is linked to a larger network over the internet. A WAN can also have MANs connected to it as well as lots of smaller LANs.

WANs are commonly used by organizations with multiple locations or branches to establish connectivity, share resources, and enable communication between widely distributed sites. The internet itself is an example of a WAN that connects networks globally.

Peer-to-peer Network

On peer-to-peer networks, all the computers on the network are equal in role, and are usually connected together in a small office or maybe at home.

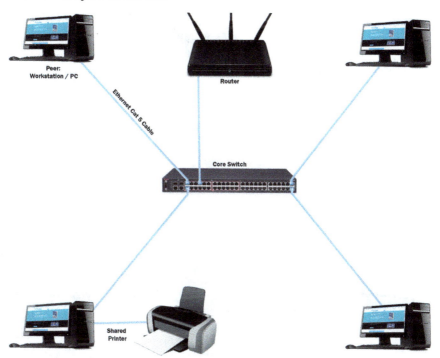

An example of a peer-to-peer network is one that might be found in a modern household, a computer in the study, one in the living room and one in the bedroom, all sharing one internet connection and one printer. Each computer, laptop, tablet or phone is called a peer.

Practically these computers are probably connected using WiFi to a switch that is built into a router provided by an ISP. They could also be connected using ethernet cables to a switch.

Each machine on the network can access the internet, and can also share files and any peripherals connected to the machine, such as a printer. PC-1 could share a folder containing files which can be accessible from the other PCs, laptops or devices.

File sharing sites such as BitTorrent are also peer to peer networks.

Client-server Network

Client-server networks are found in businesses, colleges and places you would find a lot of computers.

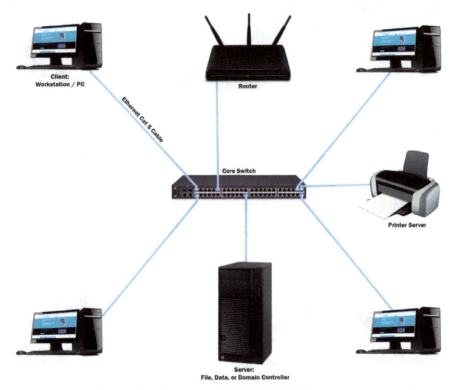

These networks consist of a number of PCs called clients located in offices on an employee's desk, in classrooms and are usually connected using CAT5 cables.

Also on the network there would be one or more servers. Servers are large computers that hold data and shared resources that are served to the client PCs on the network. Hence the name client-server. The server could store shared folders containing documents that can be accessed by all the computers on the network. The server could also provide authentication to users logging onto the network, eg in a Windows domain.

Similarly the printer would be a print server that each computer on the network has access to and can send documents to print.

Each machine can access the internet.

Network Topologies

There are various topologies used to construct networks. We'll take a look at some of the common ones that have been used in the past.

Star

In local area networks with a star topology, each node is connected to a central hub, called a switch, with a point-to-point connection.

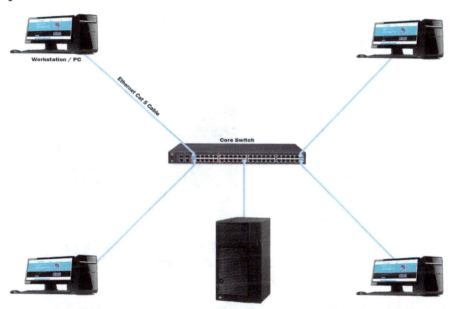

Star topologies are common on Fast Ethernet LANs where each workstation or server connects to a central switch like the one below.

An advantage of the star topology is the simplicity of adding additional nodes. The primary disadvantage of the star topology is that the switch represents a single point of failure.

Bus

In bus topologies although somewhat obsolete in favour of Fast Ethernet now days, each node is connected to a single cable called a bus.

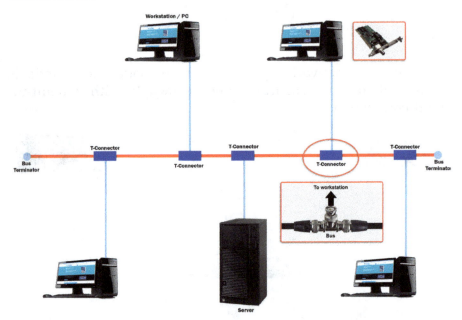

All nodes are connected to a single cable called a bus that acts as a backbone for the network. At each node on the bus you'd have a T-Connector where a workstation or server can be connected. Each node has its own connection to the bus.

To prevent reflection of the signals traveling down the bus, terminators are attached at both ends of the bus. The terminator is plugged directly into the bus cable at each end.

Each node on the network sees the data, but only the node to which the data is addressed will accept it. This leads to a "broadcast" nature for the network, where a transmission from any one node is received by all other nodes.

Since there is only one path for transmitting data, there is a chance of collision when two or more nodes try to send data at the same time. To manage this, bus networks often use a protocol such as Carrier Sense Multiple Access with Collision Detection (CSMA/CD).

Ring

Another technology that is somewhat obsolete by today's standards is the ring network which is a bus network in a closed loop. A token ring network is a common implementation, where a special packet called a token is "passed" around the ring - only the PC with the token is allowed to send data onto the ring. Have a look at the diagram below.

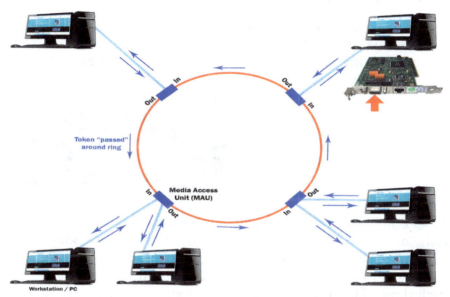

Each node on the ring has a Media Access Unit which looks something like this...

The two ports either end are for the ring coming in, and the ring going out as can be seen on the diagram at the top of the page. The ring could be coming in from another building and going out to another, while all the workstations in the building connect to the MAU.

115

Ethernet

Ethernet is a widely used networking technology that allows devices to communicate with each other over a local area network (LAN). It was developed in the 1970s by Xerox Corporation's Palo Alto Research Center (PARC) and later standardized by the Institute of Electrical and Electronics Engineers (IEEE) as the IEEE 802.3 standard.

Computers on an ethernet network are usually connected together using copper CAT 5, 6, or 7 ethernet copper cable. Copper cabling is cost-effective, suitable for shorter distances, and commonly used in smaller networks such as LANs.

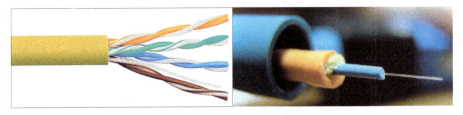

Fiber optic cables are generally more expensive and can transmit data over much longer distances, up to a several kilometers without experiencing significant signal degradation. This makes them ideal for large high speed telecommunications networks, including long-distance phone systems, internet service providers (ISPs), internet backbones, and large organizations.

Computers on an ethernet network are usually plugged into a device called a switch, shown below.

This device passes data between the different computers on the network. Ethernet switches are fundamental components in building local area networks, providing efficient and reliable data transmission between connected devices. They play a crucial role in managing network traffic, enhancing network performance, and improving overall network scalability and flexibility.

Ethernet cables connect computers to the switch using either fast ethernet (100BaseT) or gigabit ethernet (1000BaseT), and has a limit of about 100m. The cables are terminated with a standard RJ45 connector such as the one on the right.

Note there are 4 pairs of wires (orange, green, blue, brown) and 8 pins. The connectors are usually wired to the T568B standard as shown below.

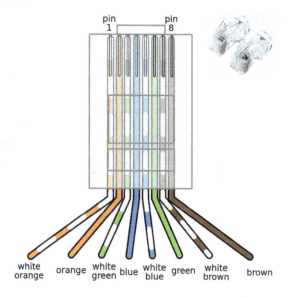

Pins 1 and 2: Transmit (+) and Transmit (-)
Pins 3 and 6: Receive (+) and Receive (-)
Pins 4, 5, 7, and 8: often used for Power Over Ethernet.

There are several types of fiber optic connectors:

SC connectors are square-shaped connectors that feature a push-pull latching mechanism. LC connectors are popular in high-density applications due to their small form factor and precise alignment. ST connectors are cylindrical connectors with a bayonet-style twist lock mechanism.

Cellular Networks

A cellular network or mobile network is a wireless network distributed over land and is divided into areas called cells. Each of these cells is assigned a set of frequencies and is served by a radio base station (labelled F1-F4 in the diagram). The frequencies can be reused in other cells, provided that the same frequencies are not reused in neighboring cells to avoid interference. Examples include GSM, 2G, 3G, 4G, and 5G.

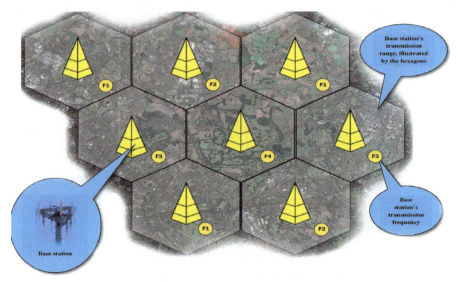

On a GSM cellular network, the frequency in each cell is divided up using a process known as time-division multiple access (TDMA). This allows large numbers of phones to connect at the same time using the same frequency channel in the cell. Each user is allocated a time slot in which they can transmit or receive. The multiplexer (mux) cycles through the time slots, allowing each user to access the channel during their allocated slot.

3G uses WCDMA, 4G uses OFDMA/SC-FDMA, and 5G uses advanced techniques like beamforming and MIMO.

WiFi

WiFi allows you to connect to a wireless network, also called a Wireless LAN and is usually broadcasting on a frequency of 2.4GHz and 5GHz radio bands.

Wireless LANs are usually password protected to keep them private and to prevent unwanted visitors using your WiFi. WiFi networks usually have a network name often called an SSID.

Dual Band or Single Band?

Dual Band wireless LANs use both 2.4GHz and 5GHz but you'll need to make sure your devices (phone, laptop, tablet and computer) are compatible with these frequencies. Some devices only broadcast on 2.4GHz and some use both, so check the WiFi specs on your devices. There is far less interference on the 5GHz band and in some cases can provide better service.

Single Band wireless LANs use either 2.4GHz or 5GHz, not both.

WiFi Extenders

The technical term is wireless repeater and if you live in a big house, these can help to cover your whole property if your WiFi router doesn't quite reach.

The idea is to position the extenders as far away from your wireless router as possible without losing too much of your signal quality. This will give you maximum range.

Wireless Standards

All wireless networks are based on the IEEE 802.11 standard.

The 802.11b standard, has a maximum raw data rate of 11 Mbps using 2.4GHz and is an out dated technology now days.

The 802.11g standard, also known as Wireless G, extended the throughput to up to 54 Mbps using the same 2.4 GHz band.

The 802.11n standard, also known as Wireless N, extended throughput over the two previous standards with a significant increase in the maximum data rate from 54 Mbps to 300 Mbps, and can be used on the 2.4 GHz or 5 GHz frequency bands.

The 802.11ac standard, broadcasts on the 5GHz band and has throughput of up to 1 Gbps and is sometimes referred to as Gigabit WiFi. This is accomplished by using wider RF bands for each channel.

IEEE Standard	Frequency	Speed	Transmission Range
802.11	2.4GHz	1 to 2Mbps	Up to 20 meters indoors but range can be affected by walls.
802.11a	5GHz	Up to 54Mbps	Up to 30 meters indoors but range can be affected by walls.
802.11b	2.4GHz	Up to 11Mbps	Up to 50 meters indoors but range can be affected by walls.
802.11g	2.4GHz	Up to 54Mbps	Up to 50 meters indoors but range can be affected by walls.
802.11n	2.4GHz/5GHz	Up to 600Mbps	Up to 70 meters indoors but range can be affected by walls.
802.11ac	5GHz	Up to 1300Mbps	Up to 40 meters indoors but range can be affected by walls.

Wireless Security

There are currently multiple standards for home WiFi: WPA, WPA2, and WPA3, WPA3 being the more recent standard. WPA Stands for 'WiFi Protected Access' and is implemented using a pre-shared key (PSK). It is commonly referred to as WPA Personal, and uses the Temporal Key Integrity Protocol (TKIP) for encryption.

WPA2 uses Advanced Encryption Standard (AES) for encryption. The security provided by AES is much more secure than TKIP, so make sure your WiFi router has WPA2-PSK encryption. WPA3 uses SAE for authentication and stronger AES encryption.

WiFi Channels

The WiFi signal on the 2.4 GHz band is divided up into 22MHz wide channels. There are usually 14 channels, although in some counties there are only 12 or 13 channels.

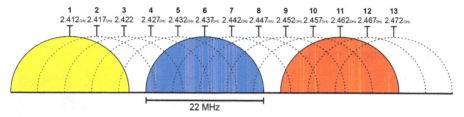

The most popular channels for 2.4 GHz Wi-Fi are 1, 6, and 11 as they don't overlap.

When WiFi access points are close together, they use these different channels so they don't interfere. Here, you can see multiple access points spread out across an office floor to provide WiFi access to all the offices.

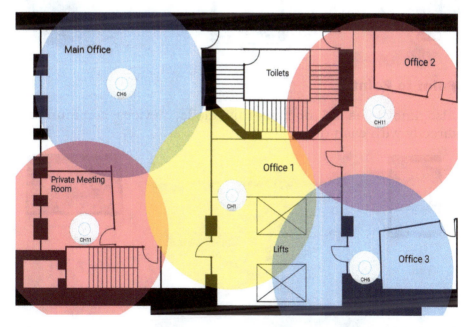

In this particular scenario, all the access points are on the same LAN. Each WiFi device, such as a laptop, will connect to the nearest WiFi access point. If you move the laptop to a different part of the building, it will switch access points.

Wireless Topologies

Much like their wired counterparts, wireless networks can be arranged in two layouts: infrastructure and point to point.

Infrastructure

Wireless devices communicate through a base station known as wireless access point.

Point to Point

Also known as ad hoc, in this mode, devices communicate directly with each other.

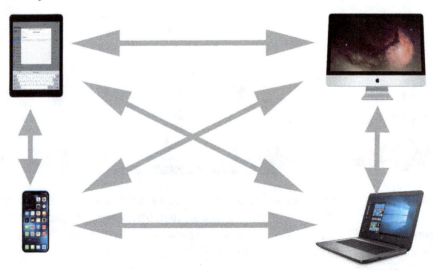

Bluetooth

Bluetooth is a wireless technology for exchanging data over short distances using a frequency of 2.4 to 2.485 GHz. This is often referred to as a PAN (or personal area network) and can be used to connect headphones, wireless mice, smart phones and make small data transfers.

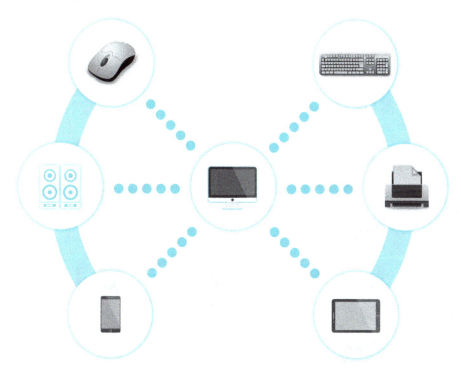

Bluetooth consumes relatively low power, making it ideal for use in portable electronic devices. Many laptops, tablets, and smartphones use Bluetooth to connect different accessories. Smartphones can even link to your car's stereo system to make a hands free kit, allowing you to safely take calls while driving.

One of the main advantages of Bluetooth technology is its convenience and ease of use, eliminating the need for cables and allowing seamless connections and communication between devices.

Bluetooth technology has evolved over the years, with newer versions offering higher data transfer rates, longer range, and improved security features.

Network Layers

The OSI 7 Layer Model is a conceptual framework used to describe the functions of a computer network and is split into seven different layers: Physical, Data Link, Network, Transport, Session, Presentation, and Application. Each layer handles a different part of the communication.

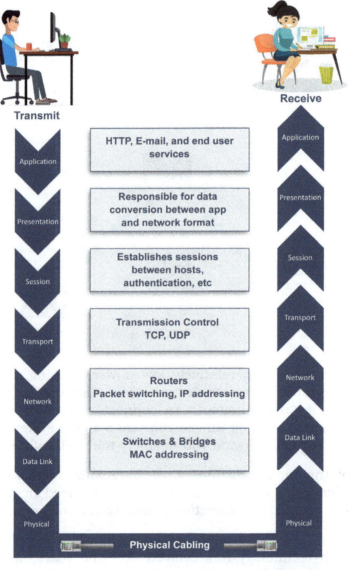

A layer serves the layer above it and is served by the layer below it.

Physical Layer (Layer 1) is concerned with transmitting raw bit streams over the physical medium. It translates data bits into electrical, radio, or optical signals. Characteristics such as voltage levels, timing of voltage changes, physical data rates, maximum transmission distances, and physical connectors are defined at this layer.

Data Link Layer (Layer 2) is responsible for node-to-node data transfer. The Data Link layer packages raw bits from the Physical layer into data frames, adding header and trailer information to create the frame structure. It also manages physical MAC addresses, network topology, error notification, frame sequencing and flow control. Network switches and protocols like PPP and Ethernet function at this layer.

Network Layer (Layer 3) oversees the delivery of packets across multiple networks. It's responsible for logical addressing, routing, and path determination. It manages network congestion and ensures that data packets are routed from the source to the destination correctly. Network routers and protocols like IP and ICMP work at this layer.

Transport Layer (Layer 4) provides the transparent transfer of data between endpoints in a network and ensures reliable data transmission. It is responsible for end-to-end error recovery, flow control, and the complete data transfer. It can also provide connection-oriented communication and multiplexing. TCP and UDP protocols operate at this layer.

Session Layer (Layer 5) sets up, coordinates, maintains, channels between applications at each end. It handles session setup, management, and teardown. Protocols like NFS, SQL, and RPC operate at this layer.

Presentation Layer (Layer 6) serves as a data translator, converting data from the Application layer into a common format before it is transmitted over the network. It's responsible for data encryption, compression, and translation services. Protocols such as SSL, TLS, JPEG, GIF, and MIME function at this layer.

Application Layer (Layer 7) is the topmost layer of the OSI model. It directly interacts with software applications and provides network services to them. Protocols such as HTTP, FTP, SMTP, and DNS operate at this layer.

5

The Internet

The Internet is a global system of interconnected computer networks linked together using the TCP/IP protocol, and evolved from a research project to develop a robust, fault-tolerant communication network back in the 1960s, known as ARPANET.

Today, you can connect to the Internet in a variety of different ways. Many of today's Internet Service Providers offer a DSL, Cable or Fibre Optic connection to the Internet, depending on where you are.

In this section, we'll take a look at some of the most common methods and their basic setups.

We'll also take a look at some of the WiFi options and basic Internet protocols.

Have a look at the video demos to help you understand. Open your web browser and navigate to the following website:

elluminetpress.com/Internet

The Internet is a network of computer networks consisting of millions of private, business, academic, and government networks. For example, the WiFi network in your home would be considered a private network. The network at school or college is an academic network. Internet access provided by an Internet Service Provider (ISP).

As you can see below, the infrastructure of the Internet consists of hardware components such as routers, switches, and cabling, as well as a suite of software protocols such as Internet Protocol (IP) and Transport Control Protocol (TCP).

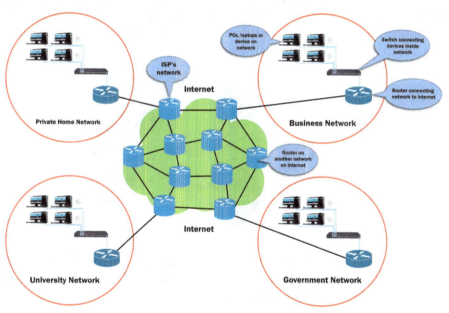

There are various Internet services and applications available. The most common being the World Wide Web. Other applications include email, FTP, video streaming, VOIP and so on.

The World Wide Web provides users with access to a vast array of documents called pages that are joined together using hyperlinks. These pages are often hosted on an organisation's website. Each website has an address, meaning the user can access these web pages by typing the address into a web browser.

Email is another popular application. Email allows users to send messages to each other. Each user is identified by an email address.

Internet Connections

There are 3 main types of Internet connection: DSL, Fibre Optic and Cable. There are others, but they are less common.

Let's go through the main options and see how they work.

Modems

Modem is short for MOdulator/DEModulator and is a device that converts digital data into an analogue signal that can be sent across a telephone line (modulation). It also converts the analogue signal it receives from the telephone line, back into digital information (demodulation).

Analog Phone Line

The modem transmits data by modulating a carrier wave to encode digital information. There are various different techniques Frequency Modulation being the simplest.

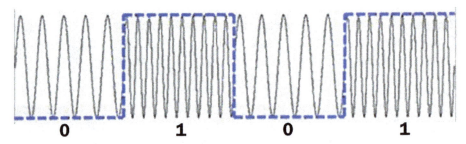

There are also other modulation techniques such as Frequency Shifted Keying and Quadrature Amplitude Modulation.

In the 80s & 90s, dial up modems were used to access the Internet.

DSL

Stands for Digital Subscriber Line and is basically implemented as **a**DSL, meaning the download speed is faster than the upload speed. This type of Internet connection connects via your telephone line, allowing you to use both your phone and Internet at the same time using a DSL filter.

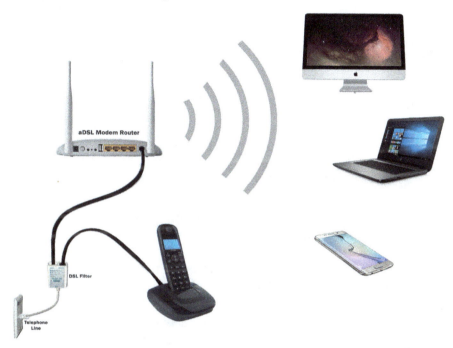

The aDSL service is be delivered simultaneously with the telephone service on the same telephone line. This is possible because the aDSL service uses higher frequency bands for data.

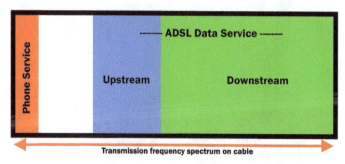

To separate the frequencies , a DSL filter is added to the line, as shown above.

Fibre Optic

In some countries, the fibre optic cable runs from the exchange to the telephone cabinet in your street and uses **v**DSL over the copper phone line to run the last 100-300m or so to your house.

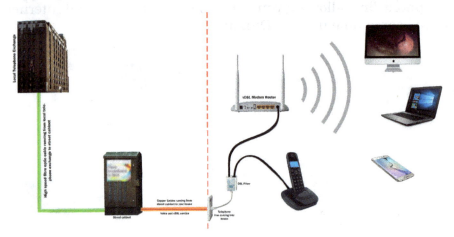

This is called FTTC or 'fibre to the cabinet' and has a very similar setup to the illustration above.

For this option to work you will need a modem router that is compatible with **v**DSL/**v**DSL2. Check with your ISP for specific details.

If you're lucky enough to can get fibre running directly to your home, this is called FTTP or 'fibre to the premises' and is set up as shown below.

This means the fibre optic cable runs from the exchange all the way to your house.

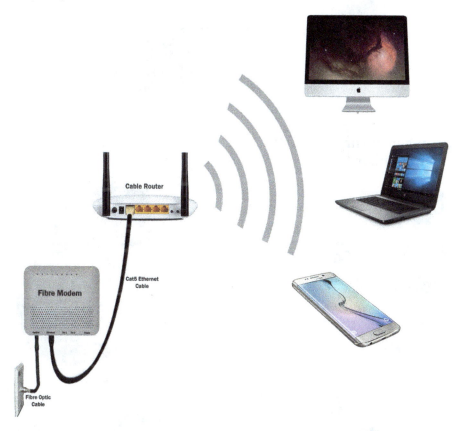

The fibre optic cable will plug into a modem supplied by your ISP which will connect you to the Internet.

You can then buy a cable router that has WiFi capabilities and plug that in using an ethernet cable. This will allow you to have WiFi in your house.

Some ISPs will already have this built into their modem, so check with them first.

All your devices such as your laptop, computer, phone, and tablet will connect to the Internet through your modem.

Cable

Cable Internet is distributed via your cable TV provider and usually runs down a COAX cable rather than a phone cable.

Setups may vary slightly from different providers, however most will be similar to the one illustrated below.

The COAX cable is split and one goes to your cable TV decoder and the other to your cable modem. From your cable modem, you can connect a cable router using an ethernet cable, which can provide WiFi. Some ISPs will already have this built into their modem, so check with them first.

Satellite

This option is available in rural areas where line based broadband services such as DSL or Fibre aren't available.

It uses a satellite dish to provide access but speeds tend to be lower and weather conditions can interfere with reception.

3G/4G/5G

This option uses the mobile/cell phone network and usually involves plugging a USB dongle with a SIM card into your computer.

3G and 4G are usually included with smart phones as part of your package or contract.

Speeds have improved over the years, however they are still slower in comparison with DSL, Cable or Fibre Optic.

Web Servers and DNS

Web servers are computers usually running Windows Server or more commonly, some flavour of the Linux Operating System such as CentOS. Running on these machines is a piece of software called a web server. This is usually Apache, IIS or NGNIX (Engine X).

In the lab demonstration below, the server on the right is running CentOS Linux and has the Apache Web Server installed. The web server is pointing at our public_html directory stored on one of the server's hard drives.

For simplicity's sake, the Apache web server is bound to port 80, which is the default port for non-encrypted connections.

The IP address of the server is 192.168.0.100.

To access the website on the your computer - the laptop, in your web browser you would need to type in 192.168.0.100. Bit of a pain, just imagine if every website you wanted to go to, you had to remember some string of numbers.

Fortunately we don't have to thanks to DNS servers, which convert our memorable domain names into IP addresses for us.

Client
192.168.1.14

Port: 5407

To keep things simple for this exercise, we wont be setting up a DNS server in the lab, but it's worth remembering the function of a DNS server on the Internet.

When you enter the domain name into your browser, your computer will send the domain name to a DNS server. The DNS server responds with the IP address (eg 192.168.0.100).

Your computer (the laptop in the illustration below), uses the IP address to connect to the web server using a port. In this case port 80.

The web server at 192.168.0.100 is listening on port 80, as it was bound to it earlier remember. You can see the configuration summary on the screen in the illustration below.

Once a connection is established, the web server then reads the HTML files in our public_html directory, and then sends the code in the index.html file to your computer - the laptop.

The browser on your computer then reads the HTML code and creates the web page on your computer.

Try it out in the lab.

Server
192.168.1.100

DHCP Servers

DHCP stands for Dynamic Host Configuration Protocol and is responsible for automatically allocating IP addresses to devices on a network.

Your Internet broadband router at home contains a DHCP server to automatically allocate each device an IP address, whether it is your phone, laptop or PC.

Devices connecting to a network broadcast a request to the DHCP server. The DHCP server sends back an IP address from its address pool along with a time period for which the allocation is valid called a lease, as well as DNS and gateway addresses, and the network's subnet mask.

Here's an example of a DHCP server running on Windows Server in our test lab. We have configured the address pool to allocate addresses from 192.168.1.1 to 192.168.1.100.

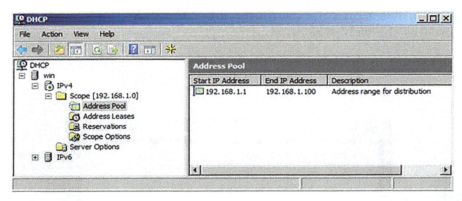

As you can see, one client has connected to the network and has been allocated an IP address.

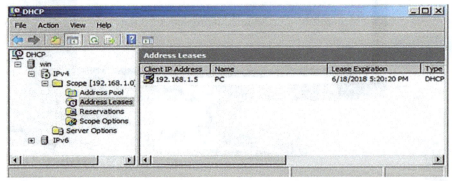

IP Addresses

An IP address identifies each device on a network. There are currently two versions of IP addressing: IPv4 and IPv6.

An IPv4 address is a 32 bit binary number divided into four 8 bit octets, and is usually expressed as a dotted decimal number. For example:

89.71.222.37

Most servers, routers, and other devices on the Internet are allocated a unique IP address (some are shared using NAT). These are known as public IP addresses and are assigned by the Internet Assigned Numbers Authority (IANA) which is currently a function of ICANN. Your ISP will assign one of these public addresses to your broadband router. Your router will then allocate a private IP address to each device that connects to your router.

The IANA have allocated the following blocks of IP addresses for private use. Most home Internet routers use class C but other larger networks can use either class A or B.

Class A	10.0.0.0 - 10.255.255.255	up to 16,777,216 devices
Class B	172.16.0.0 - 172.31.255.255	up to 1,048,576 devices
Class C	192.168.0.0 - 192.168.255.255	up to 6,5536 devices

If you type ipconfig into your command prompt in Windows, you'll see the current IP address configuration. Notice here, this machine is running on a private LAN and is using Class C private IP addressing.

```
Ethernet adapter Ethernet:

   Connection-specific DNS Suffix  . : lan
   IPv4 Address. . . . . . . . . . . : 192.168.0.133
   Subnet Mask . . . . . . . . . . . : 255.255.255.0
   Default Gateway . . . . . . . . . : 192.168.0.1
```

There are other addresses that have a specific purpose on a network.

- 0.0.0.0 represents the network itself.
- 255.255.255.255 is reserved for network broadcasts, and messages that should go to all devices on the network.
- 127.0.0.1 is called the loopback address, also called localhost meaning a device's way of identifying itself on the network.

- 169.254.0.1 to 169.254.255.254 is assigned automatically when a device can't get an address from a DHCP server.

With IPv4 you can have a maximum of 4,294,967,296 devices. Due to the rapid growth of the Internet, this address space has run out. To combat this problem, IPv6 was developed.

IPv6 uses eight 16-bit hexadecimal numbers separated by a colon. Here, we can see in the ipconfig information for this computer, and IPv6 address has been allocated.

```
Ethernet adapter Ethernet:

   Connection-specific DNS Suffix  . : lan
   IPv6 Address. . . . . . . . . . . : fdaa:bbcc:ddee:0:71a4:c9d5:57d4:ec99
   Temporary IPv6 Address. . . . . . : fdaa:bbcc:ddee:0:6165:c608:5408:c037
   Link-local IPv6 Address . . . . . : fe80::71a4:c9d5:57d4:ec49%12
```

An IPv6 address can be broken down into various parts to identify the site or organisation, network, and device. Let's take a look at the address we found using ipconfig.

The first three sets of numbers identify the organisation or site.

```
fdaa:bbcc:ddee
```

The next set of numbers identify a subnet or network within the organisation.

```
0000
```

The last four sets identify the device on the network.

```
71a4:c9d5:57d4:ec99
```

Subnets can be used to divide up large networks into more manageable smaller networks called subnets. These subnets could be departments within an organisation or faculties within a college. Home networks usually only have one subnet as they are small enough to manage.

Subnetting makes managing the network much easier than having one very large network.

TCP/IP

TCP/IP stands for Transmission Control Protocol/Internet Protocol and is a suite of communication protocols devices use to communicate over the Internet.

TCP/IP Model

The TCP/IP model, like the OSI model, uses a layered approach and has four layers.

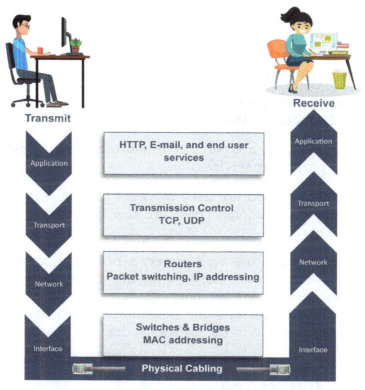

Application Layer deals with network applications such as DNS, FTP, HTTP, IMAP and SMTP. Also browsers & email programs.

Transport Layer utilizes UDP and TCP to establish connections and ensures accurate transmission of data.

Network/Internet Layer uses Internet Protocol (IP) to send packets called datagrams using packet switching.

Network Interface Layer handles the hardware (network cards etc) and physical media such as cables.

139

Ports and Sockets

A computer on a network may send data to or receive data from multiple computers at the same time. The problem is, these computers have no way of knowing which data belongs to which application. You can identify the application using a port number.

Common application layer protocols have been assigned port numbers in the range of 1 to 1023. Some common ones are:

- HTTP is port 80
- HTTPS is port 443
- IMAP is port 143
- SMTP is port 25

These ports are assigned to specific server services by the Internet Assigned Numbers Authority (IANA) a function of ICANN.

Port 1024 to 49,151 are ports an organization can register with IANA for a particular service.

Port 49,152 to 65,535 are used by client programs to assign to connections and sessions. These are also known as dynamic or ephemeral ports.

When you connect to a web server, a new TCP connection is established between the server and the client computer. The server can be listening on port 80. The TCP protocol knows which application to send the incoming data to based on the port number received in the data's header.

On the client computer, the connection is assigned a port number between 49,152 and 65,535 so that returning traffic from the server can be identified as belonging to the same connection.

The IP address and the port number form a socket. There will be a socket on the server and one on the client.

Once the socket is established, data can be transmitted between the server and client using protocols such as TCP or UDP.

We can confirm this on the client using the netstat command as shown below.

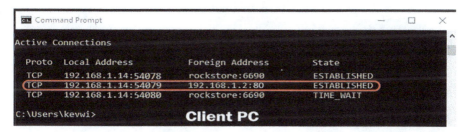

And on the server, we can confirm the connection using netstat as shown below.

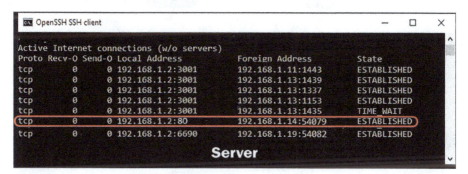

Each socket is unique and bi-directional, so applications can send and receive data.

Try typing netstat into the command prompt on a windows machine and you'll see all the current TCP connections.

Packet Switching

On a packet switched network, data is divided into small units called packets.

Remember the Internet is a global system of interconnected computer networks all linked together using routers, switches and cables, in a mesh type system where there are various different routes packets could travel. In the diagram below, each router could connect a different network and could be anywhere in the world. Each network (illustrated by the blue ellipse) could be a college, school, business, or an ISP providing Internet access to home users.

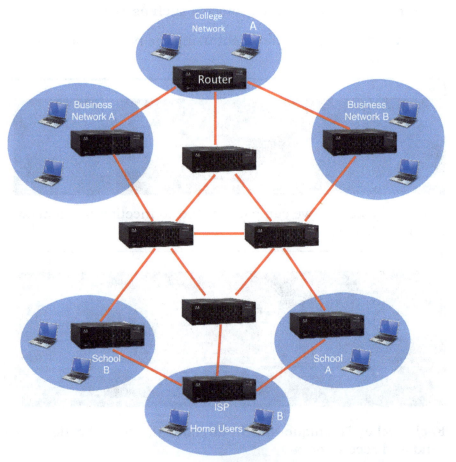

Say we are connected to the Internet using a machine on our college network (labelled A at the top of the diagram) and wanted to send an email message to someone.

The email message (or data) is divided up into packets - the number of packets depends on the size of the original data. Each packet includes a header that contains the source & destination IP addresses, total number of packets, and the packet sequence number.

For simplicity sake, lets say the message is divided up into 3 packets (illustrated by the colored envelopes in the diagram below). Each packet is sent along a different route (illustrated by the colored lines)

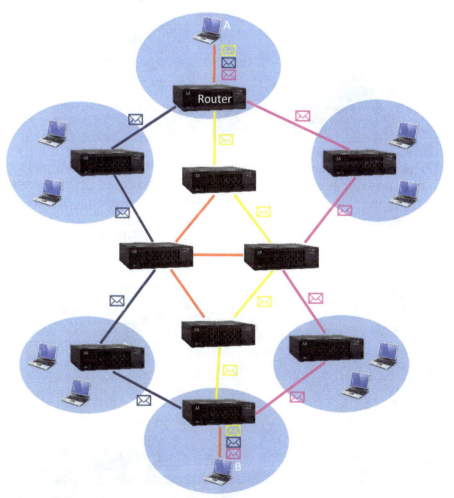

After reaching the destination through various different routes on the network, the packets are arranged in the original order according to the packet sequence number, there by reconstructing the message.

Packets

Data to be sent over the network is split into packets. This process starts at the transport layer, where data received from the application layer is divided into smaller units called segments for TCP and datagrams for UDP. Each TCP segment is assigned a sequence number for later reassembly, and a TCP header is added to each segment. The TCP header contains control information, such as source and destination port numbers.

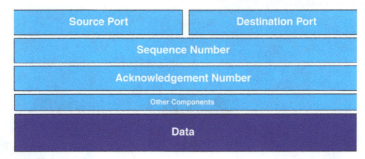

These segments (for TCP) or datagrams (for UDP) are then passed to the network layer, where they are encapsulated into packets. Each packet includes an IP header that contains necessary control information, such as the source and destination IP addresses. The actual TCP segment or UDP datagram data becomes the payload of the packet.

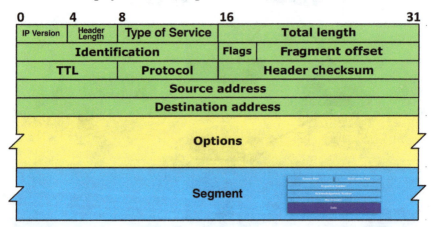

The specific fields within the packet header may vary depending on the protocol and network layer, but some common fields include the following.

Version is a 4-bit field indicates the IP version being used. For IPv4, the value is always 4.

Header Length is a 4-bit field specifies the length of the IP header in 32-bit words (4 bytes). The minimum header length is 20 bytes (5 words), and the maximum is 60 bytes (15 words).

Type of Service is an 8-bit field used for Quality of Service (QoS) purposes. It allows marking packets to prioritize or provide special treatment.

Total Length is a 16-bit field indicating the total size of the IP packet (header and data) in bytes. The minimum size is 20 bytes (header only), and the maximum size is 65,535 bytes.

Identification is used if the IP packet is fragmented, all fragments belonging to the same original packet share the same 16-bit identification number.

Flags are used for fragmentation control. The first bit is always set to 0. The second bit indicates that this packet should not be fragmented. The third bit is the More Fragments (MF) bit, set in all fragmented packets except the last one.

Fragment Offset is a 13-bit field that specifies the position of the fragment within the original fragmented IP packet.

Time to Live (TTL) has 8 bits and is decremented by 1 every time the packet passes through a router. When TTL reaches 0, the router drops the packet and sends an ICMP time exceeded message to the sender. It helps prevent packets from looping indefinitely in case of a routing loop.

Protocol is an 8-bit field that indicates the higher-layer protocol encapsulated in the IP packet. TCP has the value 6, UDP has 17, etc.

Header Checksum is a 16-bit field that stores a checksum of the IP header, allowing the receiver to detect errors in the header.

Source Address is a 32-bit field contains the source IP address of the sender.

Destination Address is a 32-bit field contains the destination IP address of the intended recipient.

IP Options field is rarely used and has a variable length based on the options applied. When used, it increases the value in the Header Length field accordingly. Examples of possible options include "source route," where the sender specifies a specific routing path.

As packets arrive at their destination device, they are processed by the Network layer. Here, the IP header of each packet is examined to ensure that the packet has arrived at the correct destination. This is done by comparing the destination IP address in the packet's header with the IP address of the receiving device.

If the data was large and had to be fragmented for transmission, the fragments arrive as separate packets. The fields in the IP header, such as Identification, Flags, and Fragment Offset, are used to reassemble these fragments back into the original datagram. All fragments belonging to the same original datagram share the same identification value, and the fragment offset value indicates where in the datagram a particular fragment belongs.

Once the packet is verified and reassembled (if it was fragmented), it is passed up to the Transport layer. This layer looks at the protocol field in the IP header to determine whether the packet payload should be processed by TCP, UDP, or another protocol.

In this example, we used the TCP protocol. So the packet payload contains TCP segments.

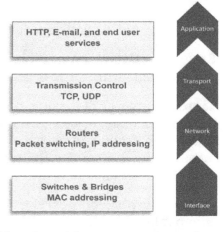

Each TCP segment includes a TCP header with a sequence number that was assigned when the data was originally segmented at the source. The TCP protocol uses these sequence numbers to reassemble the segments into the correct order. If the Transport layer protocol in use is TCP, it also has mechanisms to request re-transmission of any lost data.

Once all the segments have been reassembled into the original data, they are passed up to the Application layer, completing the journey from the source to the destination.

What is a URL?

Each web site on the World Wide Web has an address called a URL or Uniform Resource Locator. The URL itself can be broken down into its basic elements. Let's take a closer look at an example.

Protocol: The method used to access or retrieve the information from the server. When browsing the web it's usually https. With HTTPS, communication is encrypted using Transport Layer Security (TLS) or, formerly, Secure Sockets Layer (SSL).

Sub domain: Sub domains are subdivisions of the main domain that can be used to separate different areas of a website. For instance, a company might use a "blog" sub domain for its blog section (blog.elluminetpress.com) and a "shop" sub domain for its online store (shop.elluminetpress.com).

Domain name: A domain name is a unique name that identifies a website or organization. Also known as a second level domain (SLD). Each domain name corresponds to a specific IP address.

Top-Level Domain (TLD): TLDs are the highest level of domain names in the hierarchical Domain Name System (DNS) of the Internet. There are a variety of TLDs to denote the purpose or location of a website, such as ".gov" for government entities, ".edu" for educational institutions, country-specific such as ".uk" for the United Kingdom and ".com" for commercial.

Path: The path identifies a specific resource on the web server, such as a page or an image. In this case, it's pointing to the "shop" page on the website.

HTML

HTML, or HyperText Markup Language, is the standard markup language for documents designed to be displayed in a web browser. HTML is used to structure content on the web and to provide semantic meaning to that content. It is not a programming language, but a markup language that determines the structure of your content.

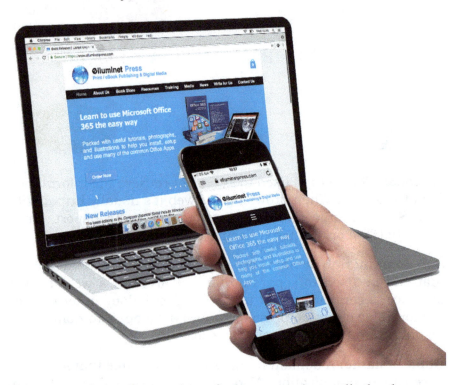

HTML consists of a series of elements that tell the browser how to display the content. These elements are represented by tags. HTML tags most commonly come in pairs for example <p> and </p> which represents a paragraph of text, or <h1> and </h1> for main headings. These tags are often used with CSS (Cascading Style Sheets) to apply styling to HTML elements and control how they are displayed on screen. JavaScript is also used to add interactivity and complex functionality to websites.

Today websites are built to adapt the layout based on the viewing environment or device such as a smart phone, laptop or desktop. This is known as responsive web design

Where are the HTML Files Stored?

On a web server, the HTML files are typically stored in a directory that is configured to be publicly accessible. In many hosting environments, particularly shared hosting, this directory is often called public_ html. However, the exact directory can vary depending on the server's configuration and the web server software being used such as Apache or Nginx.

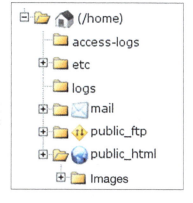

Inside the this folder, you can create subfolders to organize resources. For instance, you might have an 'images' folder to store all image files, a 'css' folder for your CSS stylesheets, and a 'js' folder for JavaScript files. This structure can help in managing and maintaining the website more effectively.

Web servers can be housed in various forms, such as rack-mounted devices in a server room or data center, or as virtual machines in a cloud environment. Each web server is assigned an IP address, which is utilized by the Domain Name System (DNS) to translate the URL typed into a web browser into an IP address that can be routed across the internet.

The operating system on a web server can vary. Some servers run on Linux distributions like CentOS, while others might use Windows Server, depending on the needs of the website and the preferences of the server administrator.

Cloud Computing

The "cloud" was originally a metaphor for the Internet, and many network diagrams represented the Internet with a symbol of a cloud.

Introduction

As Internet services advanced, the cloud evolved into a collection of hardware devices, including data servers and application servers, that provide services such as email, apps, and disk storage for documents, music, and photos. These cloud services include the delivery of software and remote storage space, minimizing the need for local storage on the user's machines.

If you have an account with a web-based email service like Hotmail or Gmail, you have already experienced the cloud. Instead of running an email program on your computer, you log into a web email account remotely. The storage for your account doesn't exist on your computer; it's in the cloud. For example, files would be stored on OneDrive for Microsoft services or Google Drive for Google services.

You can run Microsoft Word online using your tablet, laptop, or phone to edit your documents. Similarly, if you are using Google Drive, you can use Google Docs to edit your documents. All these services can be accessed through a web browser on your device.

You can also collaborate with other users, such as colleagues or friends. You can share photos or documents for them to view and edit, allowing for collaboration on projects from around the world or simply sharing the latest photo with a friend.

This has become a significant advantage as data can be stored centrally, making backups easier. Applications and servers can be built and maintained centrally by dedicated support staff, minimizing downtime.

Your files on the cloud are stored on a server in a server farm rather than locally on your computer. In the photograph below, there can be about 20 or more servers stacked up in each cabinet and hundreds of cabinets filling entire rooms, serving millions of people who subscribe to the service.

Types of Service

Cloud computing has become an essential technology for many organizations, offering various benefits such as scalability, flexibility, reduced costs, and a much smaller maintenance overhead. There are different types of cloud service. Lets take a look at what these are.

Software-as-a-service or (SaaS)

Software-as-a-Service (SaaS) is a cloud computing model in which software applications are delivered over the Internet as a service. Rather than installing and running software on their own computers or servers, users access the software through a web browser or mobile app, paying a subscription fee to the service provider.

Examples of SaaS include Adobe Creative Cloud, Microsoft 365, and Google Docs, where applications are designed for end-users and delivered over the Internet.

Platform-as-a-service or (PaaS)

Platform-as-a-Service (PaaS) is a cloud computing model in which a service provider delivers a platform for developing, running, and managing applications over the Internet. PaaS provides a complete environment for developers to build, test, and deploy applications without the need to manage the underlying infrastructure.

Examples of PaaS include Google Cloud Platform and Microsoft Azure.

Infrastructure-as-a-service or (IaaS)

Infrastructure-as-a-Service (IaaS) is a cloud computing model in which a service provider delivers computing infrastructure as a service over the Internet. IaaS provides virtualized computing resources such as servers, storage, and networking, allowing users to create and manage their own computing infrastructure in the cloud.

Examples of IaaS include Rackspace and Amazon Web Services, which provide the hardware and software that power the cloud, such as servers, storage, networks, and operating systems.

Virtual Private Networks

A Virtual Private Network (VPN) is a technology that establishes a secure, point-to-point connection between your device (such as a computer or smartphone) and another network or a VPN server over the internet. It can also be a site-to-site connection between two VPN servers.

A VPN creates a secure and encrypted connection between your device (client) and a VPN server. This encrypted connection is known as the VPN tunnel. The primary purpose of the VPN tunnel is to protect your data and ensure privacy while it travels between your device and the VPN server.

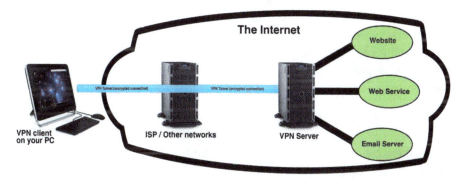

The VPN server acts as an intermediary between your device and the website you want to access there by hiding your real IP address.

When you want to access a website, your request first goes to the VPN client on your device. The VPN client encrypts this request and sends it through the VPN tunnel to the VPN server.

From the VPN server, the encrypted request is then forwarded to the website's server over the regular internet. The website's server processes the request and sends the response back to the VPN server.

Once the VPN server receives the response from the website's server, it encrypts the data and sends it back through the VPN tunnel to your VPN client on your device.

The VPN client on your device receives the encrypted response, decrypts it, and presents the website's content to you.

Internet Security

Internet security, also known as cybersecurity, is a crucial aspect of the modern digital world, involving wide a range of practices, technologies, and policies designed to protect networks, devices, programs, and data from attack. As the internet continues to evolve, so do the threats, making internet security an ever-important topic.

Common threats include malware, phishing (pronounced "fishing"), distributed denial-of-service (DDoS) attacks, and man-in-the-middle (MitM) attacks.

Malware covers a wide range of malicious software such as viruses, worms, trojans, ransomware, and spyware, each designed to cause harm or steal information. For example, WannaCry ransomware made headlines in 2017 by exploiting a vulnerability in Windows to encrypt files on infected computers, demanding ransom payments in Bitcoin to decrypt the files.

Phishing uses deception to trick individuals into divulging sensitive information, often through fraudulent emails or text messages by masquerading as a trustworthy source such as a bank, company, or authority. In 2016, the Democratic National Committee (DNC) was breached when attackers used phishing emails to gain access to email accounts, leading to the leak of sensitive information.

DDoS attacks are malicious attempts to disrupt the normal traffic of a targeted server, service, or network by overwhelming the target or its surrounding infrastructure with a flood of internet traffic. One notable example is the 2016 Dyn attack, where a massive DDoS attack used the Mirai botnet to cause widespread internet outages, affecting major websites like Twitter, Netflix, and Reddit.

MitM attacks involve a cyber attacker secretly intercepting and potentially altering the communication between two parties who believe they are directly communicating with each other. This type of attack can compromise the confidentiality and integrity of the communication, allowing the attacker to steal sensitive information, inject malicious content, or impersonate one of the parties involved. An example is the Superfish scandal in 2015, where pre-installed software on Lenovo laptops intercepted and decrypted HTTPS traffic, making users vulnerable to MitM attacks.

To combat these threats, several strategies are employed. Firewalls, both hardware and software, monitor and control incoming and outgoing network traffic based on predetermined security rules. They act as a barrier between trusted and untrusted networks, with packet filtering and stateful inspection being common methods.

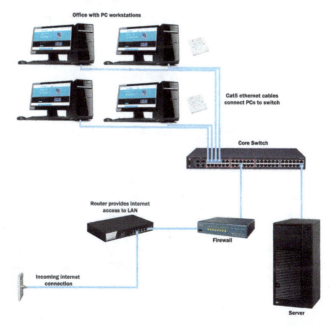

Encryption is another critical component of internet security, converting information into code to prevent unauthorized access. Protocols like SSL/TLS establish encrypted links between web servers and browsers, while end-to-end encryption ensures data is secure from the sender to the recipient.

Antivirus and anti-malware software play a crucial role in detecting, preventing, and removing malware, with real-time scanning and regular updates being essential for maintaining effectiveness.

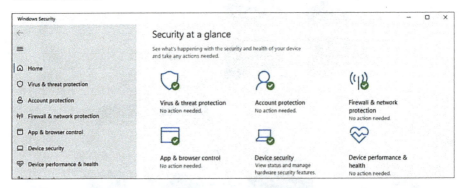

Intrusion Detection and Prevention Systems (IDPS) monitor network activities for malicious behavior, using signature-based detection for known threats and anomaly-based detection for unusual activities.

Multi-Factor Authentication (MFA) adds an extra layer of security by requiring multiple verification factors for access, beyond just a password. Regularly updating software with security patches is also vital to fix vulnerabilities that could be exploited by attackers.

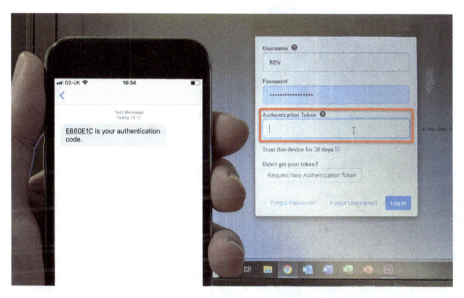

Using biometric data (such as fingerprints, facial recognition, or iris scans) for authentication provides a higher level of security compared to traditional passwords.

6 Computer Fundamentals

A computer is a machine that can store and process data according to a sequence of instructions called a program.

At their most fundamental level, these machines can only process binary data: 1s and 0s.

In this chapter, we'll take a look at using the binary code to encode data, as well as binary arithmetic and number bases.

We'll look at using logic gates to build simple circuits and how they form the building blocks for electronic devices, before moving onto the fetch execute cycle and instruction sets.

Have a look at the video demos to help you understand. Open your web browser and navigate to the following website:

elluminetpress.com/funda

Representing Data

The computer uses 1s and 0s to encode computer instructions and data. RAM is essentially a bank of switches: 'off' represents a 0 and 'on' represents a 1.

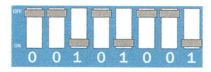

Using this idea, data can be encoded using either ASCII or Unicode and stored in RAM or on a disc drive.

ASCII code

The American Standard Code for Information Interchange (ASCII), originally used a 7-bit binary code to represent letters, numbers and other characters. Each character is assigned a binary number between 0 to 127. For example:

Capital A is 01000001_2 (65_{10})
Lowercase a is 01100001_2 (97_{10})

000-31 is reserved for control characters such as end of line, carriage returns, end of text, and so on.

032-126 covers symbols, numbers 0-9, and all lowercase and uppercase letters.

Later 8-bit character encodings were created that extended the usable character range beyond ASCII while keeping ASCII unchanged in the lower 128 values. These included mathematical symbols, international characters and other special characters needed.

Unicode

Unicode is a universal encoding standard for representing the characters of all the languages of the world, including those with larger character sets such as Chinese, Japanese, and Korean.

UTF-8 is a variable length encoding system that uses one to four bytes to represent a character. UTF-8 is backwards compatible with ASCII and widely used in internet web pages. In your HTML code you might see something like this: `<meta charset="utf-8">`.

Binary Numbers

Binary numbers only have ones and zeros, in other words you can only represent a number using a 1 and a 0. We do this using the binary or base 2 number system. Using this system we can count in binary. Here's a table to help you:

Decimal	Binary
1	0001
2	0010
3	0011
4	0100
5	0101
6	0110
7	0111
8	1000
9	1001
10	1010

With decimal numbers (or base 10), if you remember from primary school mathematics, reading from right to left you have your ones, tens, hundreds, thousands and so on. You get these by writing out your powers of 10.

$10^0 = 1$

$10^1 = 10$

$10^2 = 100$

$10^3 = 1000$

So to write the number 123, you'd have 3 'ones', 2 'tens', and 1 'hundred'. Adding these together you get 123.

100	10	1		
1	2	3	=	One 100 + Two 10s + Three 1s = 123

With binary it's the same principle, except you use 2s instead of 10s. You get these by writing out your powers of 2.

$2^0 = 1$

$2^1 = 2$

$2^2 = 4$

$2^3 = 8$

160

So to read the number $1\,1\,1\,1\,0\,1\,1_2$, reading from right to left you'd have 1 'ones', 1 'twos', 0 'fours', 1 'eights', 1 'sixteens', and so on.

You'd end up with something like this

64	32	16	8	4	2	1	
1	1	1	1	0	1	1	
64 +	32	+ 16	+8		+ 2	+ 1	= 123

Add the numbers together.

Convert Binary to Decimal

Using the principle mentioned earlier, lets try convert a number. Convert 01100110_2 to decimal.

First, write out your binary number and assign the place values.

Place value: 128 64 32 16 8 4 2 1
Device: ⓪①①⓪⓪①①⓪

Now wherever there is a 1, add the place values together. So you'll end up with something like this.

2^7	2^6	2^5	2^4	2^3	2^2	2^1	2^0
Place value: 128	64	32	16	8	4	2	1
Device: ⓪	①	①	⓪	⓪	①	①	⓪
	64+32		+		4 + 2	=	102_{10}

So, $01100110_2 = 102_{10}$

Take a look at the video demo at

elluminetpress.com/funda

Convert Decimal to Binary

To convert a decimal number to binary, continually divide the number by 2. If the number divides equally then write down 0, if there is a remainder write down 1.

Lets take a look at an example.

Convert 67_{10} to binary.

You'll end up with something like this

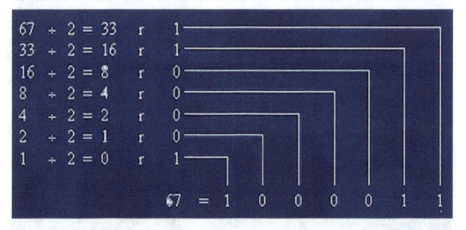

Remember, you construct the binary number reading your remainders from the last one to the first one.

Take a look at the video demo at

elluminetpress.com/funda

Binary Addition

Adding two binary numbers together is fairly straight forward. All you have to remember are these simple rules...

```
0 + 0 = 0
0 + 1 = 1
1 + 0 = 1
1 + 1 = 0 carry 1
1 + 1 + 1 = 1 carry 1
```

Have a look at adding these two numbers together, and apply the rules quoted above.

Working from the right to the left we get:
0+1=1, 0+1=1, 1+1=0 carry 1, 1+1+0=0 carry 1

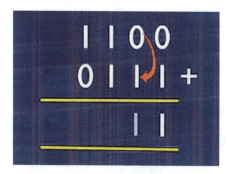

Once you work through the steps, you'll end up with something like this:

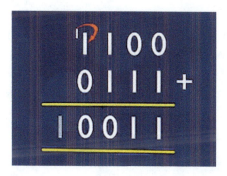

Take a look at the video demo at

elluminetpress.com/funda

Binary Multiplication

Multiplying binary numbers together is fairly straight forward. All you have to remember are these simple rules...

```
0 x 0 = 0
0 x 1 = 0
1 x 0 = 0
1 x 1 = 1
```

Lets try an example. Multiply 101 x 11

First we multiply 101 by the first 1, following the rules above.

101
  11 x
101

Then on the next line, we put a 0 as a place-holder

101
  11 x
101
    0 <-- add place-holder

Then multiply 101 by second 1, which produces 101.

101
  11 x
101
1010 +

Once you've done the that, add the two together (101 + 1010) using the binary addition rules on page 163.

101
  11 x
101
1010 +
1111

So 101 x 11 = 1111

(in decimal 5 x 3 = 15)

Binary Shift

Binary shifts are a way of multiplying or dividing binary numbers.

To multiply a number, shift all the digits in the binary number along to the left and fill the gaps after the shift with a 0. This is also known as a logical shift and is best used on unsigned binary numbers.

Lets take a look at an example:

To multiply by two, shift all digits one place to the left.

For example, 00010011_2 x 10_2 = 00100110_2
(in decimal: 19 x 2 = 38)

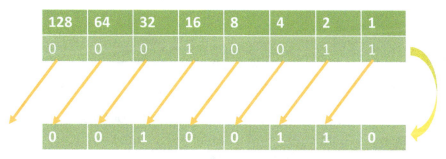

To multiply by four, shift all digits two places to the left. To multiply by eight, shift all binary digits three places to the left.

To divide a number by two, shift all the digits in the binary number one place to the right.

For example 00001011_2 / 10_2 = 00001001_2
(in decimal: 19 / 2 = 9)

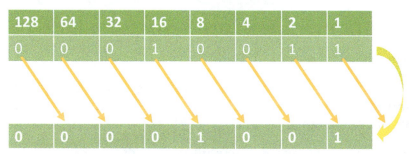

To divide by four, shift two places to the right. To divide by eight, shift three places to the right.

Now what happens if you want to multiply a binary number by 3?

00010011_2 x 11_2
(in decimal: 19 x 3 = 57)

What do we do? Well we'd have to first do a binary shift by shifting all the digits one place to the left (multiplying by 2). The closest multiplier without going over.

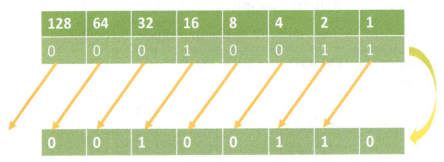

This takes us up to 00100110_2 (or 38_{10})

Next we need to add the original number 00010011 to our answer *(in decimal 38 + 19 = 57)*.

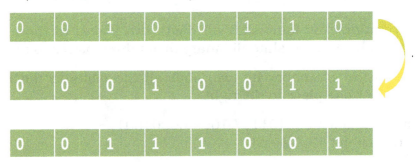

So, 00010011 x 11 = 00111001 *(in decimal: 19 x 3 = 57)*

This is called a shift and add.

You will have noticed that if you were using a logical shift to multiply numbers, you are in danger of changing the sign if you were using signed binary.

You can use an arithmetic shift to correct this problem. With an arithmetic shift, the sign bit stays the same as the data shifts. The sign bit is usually the left most bit.

Signed and Unsigned Binary

Unsigned binary numbers are positive numbers and do not require an arithmetic sign.

0011_2 unsigned is 3_{10}

1001_2 unsigned is 9_{10}

Signed numbers require an arithmetic sign. When representing a signed binary number, the bit on the far left, known as the most significant bit (or MSB), is used to represent the arithmetic sign. 0 for positive, and 1 for negative numbers.

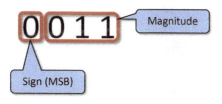

Using sign and magnitude, when a number is represented with this method, the most significant bit (MSB) represents the sign.

So...

$\mathbf{0}011_2$ is 3_{10}

and...

$\mathbf{1}011_2$ is -3_{10}

Remember, the bit on the left represents the sign.

$\mathbf{1}001_2$ is -1_{10}

One's Complement

One's complement is obtained by inverting each bit of the binary number. So, positive numbers are represented in binary form and negative numbers using one's complement notation.

For example, the number 010_2 is 101_2 using one's complement notation.

167

Two's Complement

Two's complement is a way of storing positive and negative binary integers.

The first bit on the far left is the sign bit, and is used to distinguish between positive and negative binary numbers. If the first bit is 1, then the binary number is negative, and if the first bit is 0, then the binary number is positive. The bit on the far left is also known as the most significant bit.

Here are some examples:

Negative		0	Positive	
-1	1111	1	0001
-2	1110	2	0010
-3	1101	3	0011
-4	1100	4	0100
-5	1011	5	0101
-6	1010	6	0110
-7	1001	7	0111
-8	1000	-	

Let's take a look at how we represent a number in two's complement notation. Consider the decimal number -10_{10}

To represent in two's complement, first take the normal binary representation of 10_{10}

0	0	0	0	1	0	1	0

Next invert the digits, so 0s become 1s, and 1s become 0s.

0	0	0	0	1	0	1	0

1	1	1	1	0	1	0	1

Finally add 1_2 to the number.

Add 1

1	1	1	1	0	1	1	0

So -10_{10} in two's complement binary notation is 11110110_2

168

Binary Fractions

You can express factions using the binary number system. You can express these fractions using fixed point or floating point. In fixed point, the binary point is set in a fixed position. With floating point, the location of the point moves around.

Unsigned fixed point		Integer	Fraction	
Signed fixed point	Sign	Integer	Fraction	
Floating point	Sign	Exponent	Sign	Mantissa

Fixed Point

In decimal, the digit immediately to the right of the decimal point is worth one tenth (1/10), then a hundredth (1/100), a thousandth (1/1000), and so on.

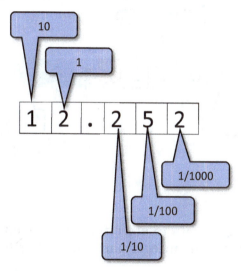

In binary, it's the same idea, except the first digit to the right of the point is a half, the next is a quarter, then an eighth and so on.

+/-	2	1	.	$\frac{1}{2}$	$\frac{1}{4}$	$\frac{1}{8}$	$\frac{1}{16}$	$\frac{1}{32}$	$\frac{1}{64}$
0	1	0	.	1	0	1	0	0	0

There are three parts to a fixed-point number: the sign, the integer, and the fraction.

169

The first bit on the left is the sign bit if using signed binary and indicates whether the number is positive or negative. The next part is the integer itself followed by a binary point. The part on the right is the fraction.

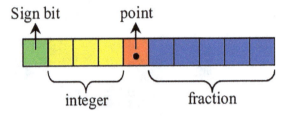

We can represent these numbers using signed binary, one's complement or two's complement. Two's complement is the preferred method.

For example, we can express a binary fraction as 0011.101_2

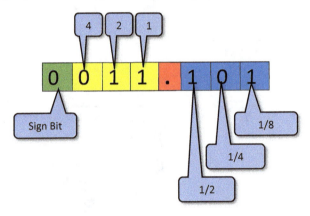

If we were using 32-bits to store the value, 1 bit is reserved for the sign, 15 bits for the integer part and 16 bits for the fractional part.

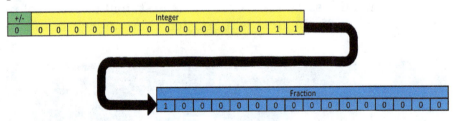

The advantage of a fixed-point system is performance but it has a limited range of values that they can be represented.

Floating Point

Floating point numbers are those that contain floating decimal points such as 88.87, 955.35, 0.06.

For example, the number 454.75 can be expressed as

4.5475×10^2

4.5475 is called the mantissa. The 2 is the exponent (this tells you where to move the decimal point), and 10 is the number base (in this case decimal base 10). Similarly 0.0025 can be expressed as

2.5×10^{-3}

In binary it's the same concept.

The binary number 1100.101 is represented as 1.100101×2^3

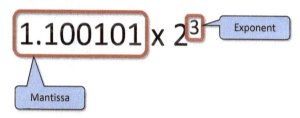

The exponent tells us to move the point 3 places to the right. If the exponent is negative, we move the point to the left.

$$1.\overset{3}{\overbrace{100}}101$$

$$1100.101$$

So 1100.101 is 1.100101×2^3

Signed integers and exponents are represented using either signed binary, one's complement, or two's complement.

As we are using 32-bits to store the number, we use 1 bit as the sign bit (or MSB), 8 bits for the signed exponent, and 23 bits for the mantissa.

MSB	EXPONENT								MANTISSA																						LSB
1	0	0	0	0	0	0	0	0	0	0	0	0	0	0	0	0	0	0	0	0	0	0	0	0	0	0	0	0	0	0	0

Convert Binary Fraction to Decimal

If you want to convert to decimal, for example convert:

0011.101_2 to decimal

First follow the same procedure as for whole binary numbers for the left side of the point (0011_2). Working from right to left we get:

4	2	1
0	1	1

$1 \times 1 + 2 \times 1 = 3_{10}$

For the right side of the point ($.101_2$), use the same idea for whole numbers, except we use fractions. Working from left to right we get:

1/2	1/4	1/8
1	0	1

So, for the fractional part $.101_2$ we end up with:

$$1 \times \frac{1}{2} + 0 \times \frac{1}{4} + 1 \times \frac{1}{8}$$

Next convert the fractions to decimals (1_{10} divided by $2_{10} = 0.5_{10}$):

$$\frac{1}{2} = 0.5$$

Anything multiplied by 0 is always 0, so we can ignore the 1/4

The next one is 1_{10} divided by 8_{10}

$$\frac{1}{8} = 0.125$$

Add them together and we get:

$$0.5 + 0.125 = 0.625$$

Now add the fraction part back to the whole number we got from the left side of the point:

$$3 + 0.625 = 3.625$$

So, 10.101_2 is 3.625_{10}

172

Hexadecimal Numbers

Hexadecimal is used as a shorthand for binary and uses the decimal numbers 0-9 and the first 6 letters of the alphabet.

Hexadecimal	Decimal
0	0
1	1
2	2
3	3
4	4
5	5
6	6
7	7
8	8
9	9
A	10
B	11
C	12
D	13
E	14
F	15

Convert Decimal to Hexadecimal

To convert a decimal number to hexadecimal, you divide the decimal number by 16, noting the remainder.

For example, lets convert 1500_{10} to hexadecimal.

First, divide 1500 by 16

1500 / 16 = 93 (ignore the decimal point)

To find the remainder, multiply your answer by 16

93 x 16 = 1488

Subtract the answer you get from 1500

1500 - 1488 = 12

The remainder is 12

So, going back to our conversion we can write:

```
1500 / 16 = 93 r 12
```

Next, divide 93 by 16

```
93 / 16 = 5
```

Find the remainder

```
5 x 16 = 80
```

Subtract the answer you get from 93

```
93 - 80 = 13
```

The remainder is 13

Going back to our conversion we get

```
93 / 16 = 5 r 13
```

Write it under the previous divide step

```
1500 / 16 = 93 r 12
```

```
93 / 16 = 5 r 13
```

We can't divide 5 by 16 so we can stop there...

Now, read off the number starting with the answer from the last divide step, then all other remainders from the bottom up. So in this example, we get:

```
5, 13, 12
```

Remember we're converting to hexadecimal, so the number 13_{10} is D, and the number 12_{10} is C.

We end up with:

$$1500_{10} = 5DC_{16}$$

Take a look at the conversion video demos. Open your web browser and navigate to the following website:

```
elluminetpress.com/funda
```

Convert Hexadecimal to Decimal

To convert your hex number, reading from right to left you mark the hex number 1, 16, 256, 4096... These are called place values.

Lets convert $5DC_{16}$ to decimal.

First, write out your hex place values like this:

	16^3	16^2	16^1	16^0
Place Value	4096	256	16	1

Underneath, write down your hex number (shown in red below). Remember D_{16} is 13_{10} and C_{16} is 12_{10}. So we write the number in like this:

	16^3	16^2	16^1	16^0
Place Value	4096	256	16	1
		5	13	12

Now, multiply each number you wrote down by the place value above it.

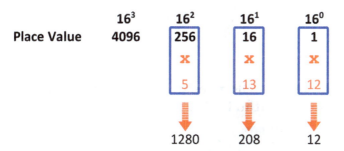

Add the results of the multiplications together.

➡ 1280 + 208 + 12 = 1500_{10}

$5DC_{16} = 1500_{10}$

Take a look at the video demo at

elluminetpress.com/funda

Boolean Logic

Boolean Logic or Boolean Algebra is the branch of mathematics, where values of variables are either true or false (1 and 0 respectively), as first described by 19th Century mathematician George Boole. This concept forms the basis for the development of computer electronics. Let's start with the basic logic gates.

AND Gate

An AND gate has two inputs. AND gates require both inputs to be 1 for the output to be 1. Expressed as `Out = A.B`

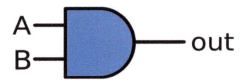

The truth table would be

A	B	Output
0	0	0
0	1	0
1	0	0
1	1	1

OR Gate

The OR gate has two inputs. OR gates require either one or both inputs to be 1 for the output to be 1. Expressed as `Out = A+B`

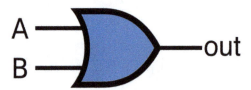

The truth table would be

A	B	Output
0	0	0
0	1	1
1	0	1
1	1	1

XOR Gate

Known as an exclusive OR gate, this gate requires the input to be either 1 or 0, not both. If both inputs are the same, the output is 0.

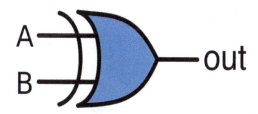

The truth table would be

A	B	Output
0	0	0
0	1	1
1	0	1
1	1	0

Expressed as Out = A⊕B

NOT Gate

A NOT gate has just one input. The NOT gate simply negates the input. So if the input is 1, the ouput is 0.

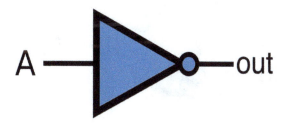

The truth table would be

A	Output
0	1
1	0

Expressed as Out = $\bar{A}$

NAND Gate

Known as a negated AND gate, this gate gives the opposite output to an AND gate.

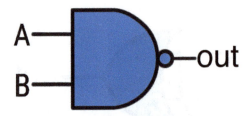

The truth table would be

A	B	Output
0	0	1
0	1	1
1	0	1
1	1	0

Expressed as Out = $\overline{A.B}$

NOR Gate

Known as a negated OR gate, this gate gives the opposite output to an OR gate.

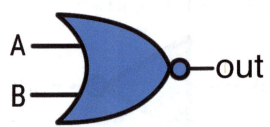

The truth table would be

A	B	Output
0	0	1
0	1	0
1	0	0
1	1	0

Expressed as Out = $\overline{A+B}$

Putting it Together

That's all well and good, but what does it all mean? Why bother? Well it turns out that these logic gates can be used to build electronic circuits. Logic gates form the building blocks used to create all sorts of electronic devices, from phones, tablets, watches, and cameras, to computers, workstations, and servers. Logic gates can be built using transistors.

Using the logic gates above we can construct a little circuit that adds two numbers. Remember electronics and computers only understand 1s and 0s so we'll add two binary numbers

$$1_2 + 1_2 = 10_2$$

In the above circuit, if we set input A to 1 and input B to 1, we would get the sum of 0, carry 1.

Using the truth table, the logic on the XOR gate would be

A	B	Sum
1	1	0

On the AND gate

A	B	Carry
1	1	1

So the answer would be sum 0, carry 1. We could write that out in binary, which would be 10_2 which is 2 in decimal.

4	2	1
0	1	0

This circuit is known as a half adder.

Using these logic gates, we can start to build circuits. Say we wanted to build a simple burglar alarm system. We could have three inputs:

- A (a master on/off switch to arm and disarm the alarm)
- B (a door/window sensor)
- C (a motion sensor in a room)

Once the alarm is on, either sensor A or B can trigger the alarm.

What logic gates do we need? Well, the word 'or' in the specification above should give you a clue as to one of them: an OR Gate.

What else? The system has an on/off switch, so we can interpret this as: the system has to be ON (A) <u>AND</u> either B OR C must be ON to trigger the alarm. So we'll also need an AND gate.

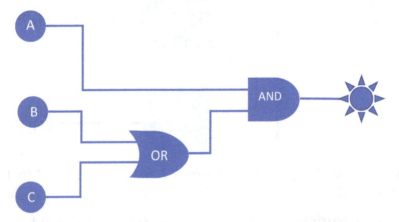

Now test the circuit with a truth table. Does it work as specified?

A (master)	B (door sensor)	C (motion sensor)	Alarm Sounds?
0	0	0	0
0	0	1	0
0	1	0	0
0	1	1	0
1	0	0	0
1	0	1	1
1	1	0	1
1	1	1	1

Have a look at the logic demos at:

elluminetpress.com/funda

180

Harvard Architecture

In early computer systems, instructions and data were stored on punch cards or punched paper tape. The photograph below is the Harvard Mark I built by IBM in 1944.

The Mark I read its instructions from a punched paper tape. A separate tape contained data for input. This separation of data and instructions is known as the Harvard architecture.

Here in the diagram below, you can see on the Harvard architecture, there is a separate area for program instructions and another for data.

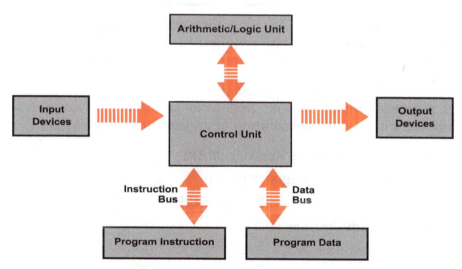

Many embedded systems in use today are based on the Harvard architecture.

Von Neumann Architecture

Von Neumann architecture is based on the stored-program computer concept, where program instructions and data are stored in the same memory.

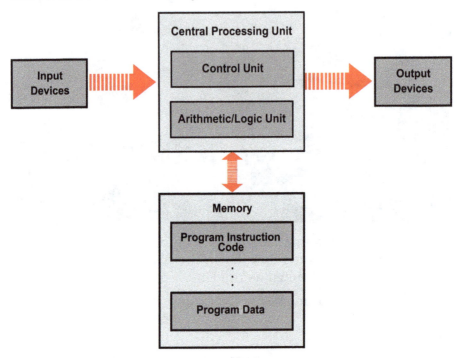

Instructions are fetched from memory one at a time and executed by the processor. Any data required by the program is fetched from memory, and any result from the execution is stored back in memory.

A processor based on Von Neumann architecture has several registers used during execution of an instruction, these are:

- Memory Address Register (MAR)
- Memory Data Register (MDR)
- Current Instruction Register (CIR)
- Program Counter (PC)
- Accumulator (ACC)

The registers and key elements of the Von Neumann architecture are used during the fetch-decode-execute cycle.

Fetch Execute Cycle

The fetch-execute cycle is the logical sequence of steps that a CPU follows to execute instructions of a program stored in memory (RAM). To demonstrate this cycle, we'll use a very simplified CPU and memory. Many modern CPUs are far more complex, and have extra features such as caches, hyper-threading and so on. Our little system will look something like this...

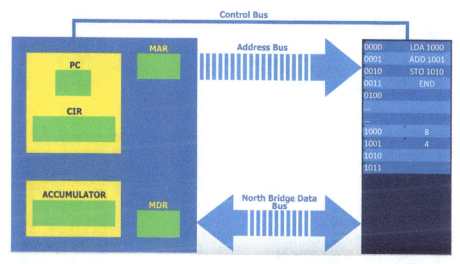

The CPU is made up of a control unit that controls the program counter (PC). This counter increments in sequence to indicate the address of the next instruction to be called from memory.

We also have a current instruction register (CIR) to hold the instruction currently being executed, and an accumulator to temporary store the result. Memory Address Register (MAR) stores the address of the next data or instruction to be accessed from or written to memory. Memory Data Register (MDR) temporarily holds the data that is being read from or written to the computer's main memory (RAM).

Lets look at en example. Below is a little program that adds two numbers together and stores the result back in memory.

```
LDA 1000 # loads accumulator with data at address 1000
ADD 1001 # adds data stored at address 1001
STO 1010 # stores result in memory at address 1010
```

Lets take a look at executing the first instruction stored in memory: LDA 1000

183

1. Fetch Phase: Copy PC to MAR.

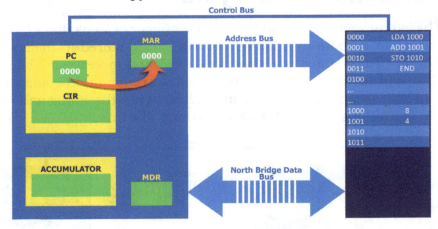

2. Copy instruction from memory (at address in MAR) to MDR.

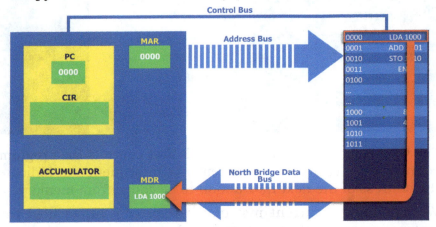

3. Copy instruction in MDR to CIR.

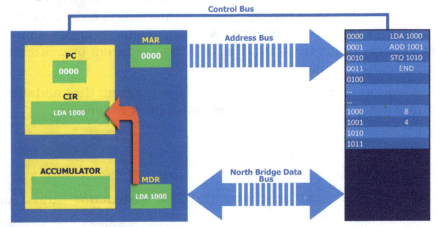

4. Increment the PC.

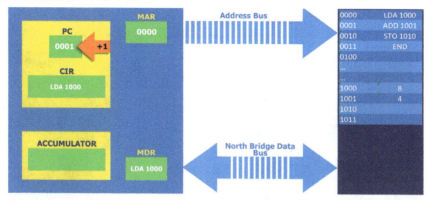

5. Decode Instruction. Strip to opcode (LDA) & operand (1000).

6. Execution phase: What does the instruction do? Well in this case, LDA is telling the CPU to load some data from an address. How do we get data from an address? Copy the operand part of instruction (1000) from CIR to the MAR.

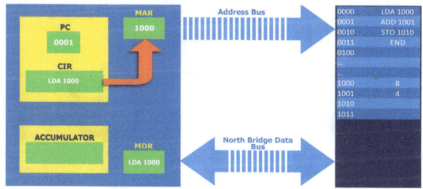

The data from address 1000 comes back over the data bus to the MDR.

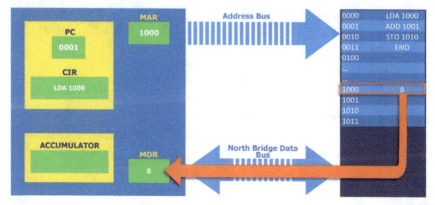

Now we have the data from the address in memory, we can carry out the instruction (add 8 to the accumulator).

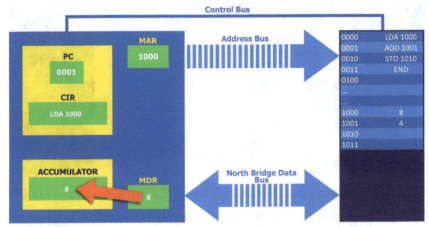

Got it? Try running the next instruction. ADD 1001

Here's the sequence of steps to help you.

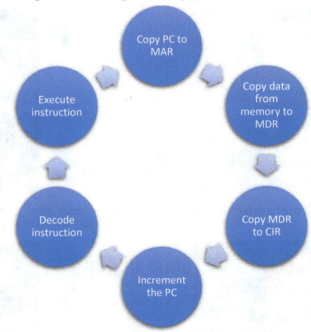

If you get stuck, take a look at the video demos to see the sequence in action. Open your web browser and navigate to the following website.

elluminetpress.com/funda

Instruction Sets

An instruction set is the complete set of all the instructions that can be executed by a processor. There are two main types: Reduced Instruction Set Computer (RISC) and Complex Instruction Set Computer (CISC).

RISC

The RISC architecture employs a simpler set of more general instructions, with each instruction typically executed in one clock cycle. RISC instructions are designed to be simple and uniform, allowing for high performance through pipelining and efficient use of registers. For example, to add two numbers, you could use assembly language instructions such as LDR for load, ADD for addition, and STR for storing the result back to memory, as well as involving various CPU registers (R1, R2, R3 etc).

```
LDR R1, [1000]    ; Load value from memory address 1000 into register R1
LDR R2, [1001]    ; Load value from memory address 1001 into register R2
ADD R3, R1, R2    ; Add values in R1 and R2, store the result in R3
STR R3, [1010]    ; Store value from R3 into memory address 1010
```

These are known as reduced instructions. RISC processors are used in many smartphones, tables, and devices which use ARM processors. Apple Silicon Macs (such as M1 etc) use RISC.

CISC

The CISC architecture uses more complex instructions, where a single instruction can execute several operations, such as loading data from memory, performing an operation, and storing the result back to memory. This reduces the number of instructions per program but increases the complexity of each instruction. For example, here the ADD instruction might carry out the loading of data, the operation, and storing the result back to memory in a single instruction:

```
ADD 1000, 1001, 1010
```

This is known as a complex instruction.

Most modern desktop and laptop computers, including PCs and Intel Macs, use the CISC architecture found in Intel and AMD processors.

Data Compression

Data compression involves encoding data using fewer bits than the original, thereby reducing the overall size. Data is usually compressed for storage or transmission over a network.

A method of data compression can be either lossy or lossless.

Lossy & Lossless

Lossy compression methods remove unnecessary or redundant data and is used to compress multimedia files such as photos, videos and audio. Some examples: JPEG images, MP4 videos, MP3 audio

MP3s are compressed using a technique called psycho acoustic compression which is based on how humans hear sounds. For example, a quiet sound immediately following a loud sound is often not heard, so the quiet sound can be removed. Also any audio that falls outside the human audible range of 20Hz to 20Khz can be removed.

Lossless compression methods reduce the file size without removing any data, so the file can be fully reconstructed when decompressed. Some examples are: ZIP

Huffman Coding

Huffman coding is a lossless data compression algorithm based on the frequency of occurrence of a data item. Codes of different lengths are assigned to characters based on the frequency of occurrence. Smaller codes are assigned to characters that have the highest occurrence.

Lets look at an example. Let's encode the string LEMMONS

First, create a table showing the frequency. Order the table by frequency from lowest to highest.

Char	Freq
S	1
N	1
O	1
E	1
L	1
M	2

Now construct a Huffman tree. Create leaves for each of your characters using the table above.

Take the first two characters from your list (S & N). Pair them together, add the frequencies. 'S' appears once, 'N' appears once, so frequency is 2. Put them back in the list based on their frequency. *Remember, the frequencies must be in order, the combined frequency is 2, so it goes after 'M' whose frequency is 2.*

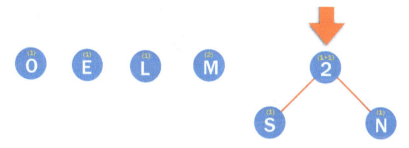

Take the next two characters from your list (O & E), pair them, add the frequencies, put them back in the list in order.

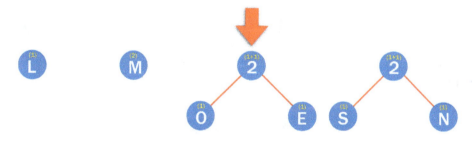

Take the next two characters from your list (L & M), pair them, add the frequencies. Add the node back into the list in order. The frequency is 3, so it goes at the end.

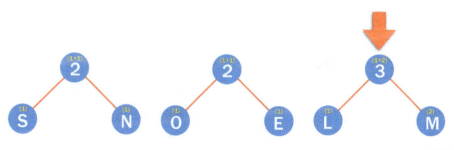

Now, take the next two from your list - nodes (S&N and O&E). Pair them, add the frequencies (2 + 2 = 4).

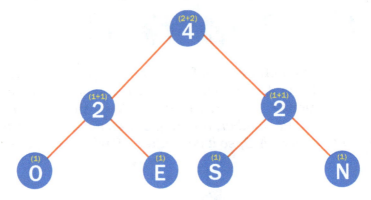

Put back in the list. Frequency is 4 so it goes at the end after node (L&M).

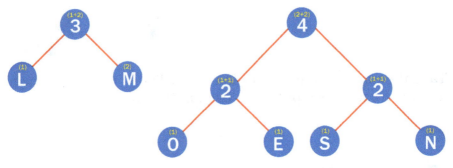

Take the next two from the list, pair them, add the frequencies (3 + 4 = 7).

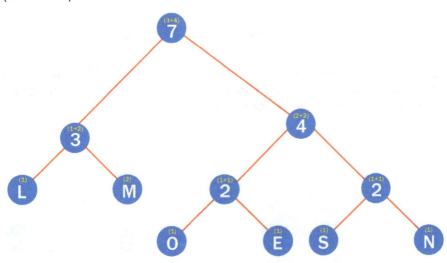

Now to encode the data you need to label the branches.

- Left branches are 0
- Right branches are 1

Each character that appears in the tree is assigned a unique code (a sequence of 0s and 1s) obtained by following the path from the root of the tree to the leaf containing the character.

So to encode a character you traverse the tree from the top node. Note the pattern of 1s & 0s until you reach the character. For example, E would be encoded as 101

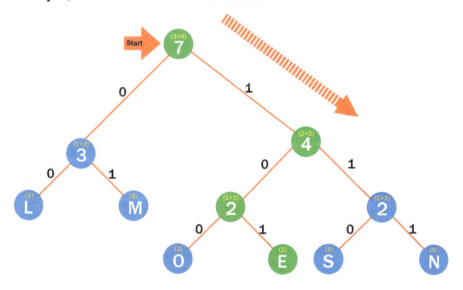

L would be encoded as 00

M would be encoded as 01

O would be encoded as 100

N would be encoded as 111

Using Huffman, LEMMONS would be encoded as

00 101 01 01 100 111 110

The original data encoded in ASCII would be:

01001100 01000101 01001101 01001101 01001111 01001110 01010011

So instead of needing 56 bits (7 bytes), with Huffman compression you only need 18 bits. You'd also have to store the tree as a translation table in order to decompress the data.

Decoding the tree, you work the opposite way.

Decode 111. To do this we go to the tree. Start from the top and traverse the tree. Turn left for a 0, turn right for a 1.

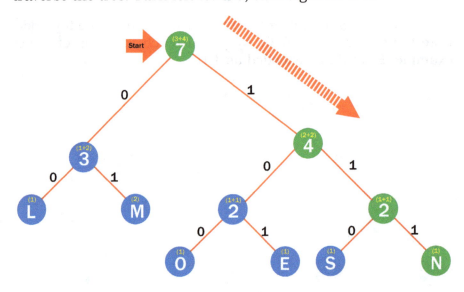

111 is N. What about 101?

Take a look at the 'huffman' coding section of the video demos. Open your web browser and navigate to the following website.

elluminetpress.com/funda

Huffman coding was developed by David A. Huffman in 1952. The idea behind Huffman coding is to assign shorter codes to more frequently occurring characters or symbols, and longer codes to less frequently occurring ones. This results in a smaller and more efficient representation of the data

Huffman coding is most effective when applied to data with significant variations in symbol or character frequencies. If the data contains characters or symbols that occur with equal frequencies, the compression benefits are limited. This technique is widely used in image, video and audio compression among various other applications.

Run Length Encoding

Run length encoding is a lossless data compression algorithm usually used to compress repetitive data. The aim is to reduce the number of bits used to represent a set of data.

The compression process involves counting the number of consecutive occurrences of each character (called a run).

Let's have a look at an example.

aaaaaaaabbbbbbcc

We can encode this as

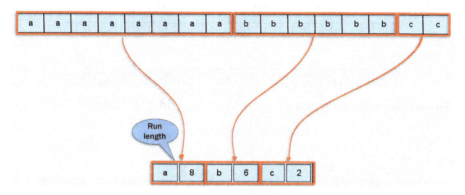

aaaaaaaabbbbbbcc would be encoded as a8 b6 c2

Encoded in ASCII the data stream would be 16 bytes.

```
01100001 01100001 01100001 01100001
01100001 01100001 01100001 01100001
01100010 01100010 01100010 01100010
01100010 01100010 01100011 01100011
```

Using RLE, the data stream would be 6 bytes.

```
01100001 00001000 01100010 00000110
01100011 00000010
```

RLE is particularly well suited to palette-based bitmap images such as the Windows Bitmap (BMP) file format.

It's worth noting that RLE's compression efficiency is limited, especially for data that lacks repetitive patterns or long runs of identical values.

Data Encryption

Data encryption is a method of keeping data secure in storage or when transmitted, where the data is encoded using an encryption key, and can only be decrypted by a user with the correct key.

The un-encrypted data is called plaintext, and the encrypted data is called a ciphertext.

To demonstrate how encryption works, we'll use a very simple technique called a Caesar cipher.

With Caesar ciphers, each letter in the plaintext is replaced by a letter a fixed number of positions down the alphabet.

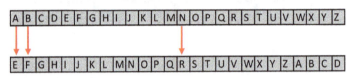

So to encrypt the word BANANA, you would get FERERE

B A N A N A

F E R E R E

Another way to encrypt data is to use a Vernam cipher. With this scheme, each plaintext character is mixed with one character from a key. This is achieved by applying the logical XOR operation to the individual bits of plaintext and the random key. See page 177 for the XOR truth table.

So to encrypt the word BANANA

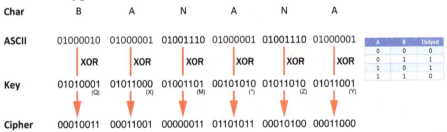

Char	B	A	N	A	N	A
ASCII	01000010	01000001	01001110	01000001	01001110	01000001
	XOR	XOR	XOR	XOR	XOR	XOR
Key	01010001 (Q)	01011000 (X)	01001101 (M)	00101010 (*)	01011010 (Z)	01011001 (Y)
Cipher	00010011	00011001	00000011	01101011	00010100	00011000

A	B	Output
0	0	0
0	1	1
1	0	1
1	1	0

Plaintext would be (BANANA):
01000010 01000001 01001110 01000001 01001110 01000001

Cipher would be (‖ ⊦ ∟ k ¶ ↑):
00010011 00011001 00000011 01101011 00010100 00011000

194

Sorting Algorithms

A sorting algorithm is simply an algorithm that puts elements of a list in a certain order.

Bubble Sort

Bubble Sort compares all the element one by one and sort them based on their values. Take the list:

```
21, 6, 2, 15
```

If we want to bubble sort this list into ascending order, we start by comparing the first number with the second number.

21
6   Compare. If first number > second number, swap

2

15

If the first number is greater than the second number, we swap the numbers.

6
21   Swap

2

15

Repeat the process with the second, third, and forth element, until you get to the end of the list.

Then we go through the list again and repeat the process. You'll need to go through the list as many times as it takes until they're all in order.

So once complete, you'll end up with:

```
2, 6, 15, 21
```

This type of sort is inefficient.

Merge Sort

A merge sort is more efficient than a bubble sort. The merge sort repeatedly divides the list in half, until each list consists of a single item. The single list items are then merged together so that they are in order. Let's look at an example.

First divide the list into the smallest items (ie divide the list in half and half again until you're left with individual items).

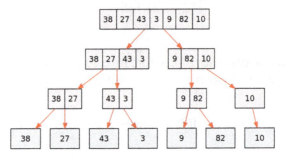

Once you have the individual items, merge and order the list back together. If you're sorting in ascending order, swap the items if the first one is bigger than the second one, see below:

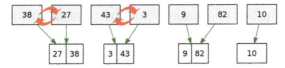

Merge the next list back together. Take item 1 from the first list and compare it with item 1 of the second list. If it's smaller put it in the new list

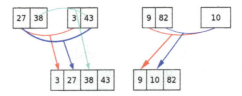

Do the same with the next lists, until you have a merged list.

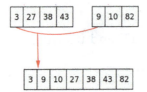

Data Storage Units

Much like length can be measured in metres and kilometres or weight in grams and kilograms.

For example, you'd have 1000 meters in a kilometre, or 1000 grams in a kilogram.

Computer storage is measured in the same fashion using bytes and kilobytes.

Technically 1 kilobyte is exactly 1024 bytes because computers operate in binary (2, 4, 8, 16, 32, 64, 128, 256, 512, 1024), but in order to simply things, 1024 is rounded off to 1000. So 1 kilobyte = 1000 bytes. These are called decimal units according to the International System of Units (SI) definition.

Decimal units such as kilobyte (KB), megabyte (MB), and gigabyte (GB) are commonly used to express the size of data. Disk drive manufacturers use the decimal system when labelling the capacity of their drives.

Unit	Size in Bytes	Abbr
KiloByte	1,000	KB
MegaByte	1,000,000	MB
GigaByte	1,000,000,000	GB
TeraByte	1,000,000,000,000	TB
PetaByte	1,000,000,000,000,000	PB

Binary units of measurement express the size of data more accurately. The International Electrotechnical Commission (IEC) created binary unit prefixes in 1998 in order to reduce the confusion.

Unit	Size in Bytes	Abbr
KibiByte	1,024	KiB
MebiByte	1,048,576	MiB
GibiByte	1,073,741,824	GiB
TebiByte	1,099,511,627,776	TiB
PebiByte	1,125,899,906,842,620	PiB

RAM is usually measured using the binary prefixes and most operating systems report the size of the data using the binary units.

This is why a hard disk labelled 500GB looks like 465GiB when you plug it in. The drive manufacturer is using the decimal units to express 500GB, but as you can see below, the operating system is using the binary units: 500GB = 465GiB.

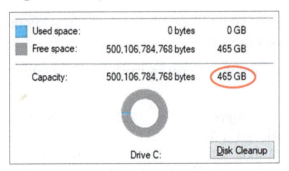

Different types of storage media have different sizes. Here are a few examples of data storage sizes.

Floppy disks, which are somewhat obsolete these days, held 1.44MB of data, probably the size of a small word document.

USB memory sticks vary in size and can be anywhere between 1GB and 512GB.

A hard disk drive can store over 1 TB of data.

Music and photos can be a couple of mega bytes each but can take up a few hundred gigabytes if you have a lot. Large documents can be around 40 megabytes, or about 50 kilo bytes if they are short.

Data Transfer Rates

Data transfer rate, also known as data rate or bandwidth, refers to the amount of data that can be transmitted over a network, from a disk drive or other device in a given amount of time.

Lets say I had an internet connection of 40mbps (megabits per second) and wanted to download a 70mega**byte** file. First you need to make sure both units are the same. Since the file is measured in mega**bytes**, you need to convert the connection speed of 40mega**bits** per second to mega**bytes** per second.

40 mega**bits** per second ÷ 8 = 5 mega**bytes** per second

So how long will it take to download?

To calculate this use

time to download = file size ÷ data rate

So...

Time to download = 70MB ÷ 5MBps (Mega Bytes per second)
                        = 14 seconds

What about a 5 Giga**byte** file?

Since we are using Mega**bytes** per second to measure the speed of the connection, we need to convert Giga**bytes** to Mega**bytes**.

5GB x 1024 = 5120 Mega**bytes** (remember the units need to be the same; can't use gigabytes and megabytes)

5120MB ÷ 5 Mega**bytes per second = 1024 seconds** (no one quotes that many seconds so you can divide this by 60 to get minutes)

1024 seconds ÷ 60 = approx 17 mins

MBps = Mega Bytes per second

Mbps = Mega Bits per second.

So when your broadband provider boasts "40meg" it is actually 40 mega**bits** per second, not 40 mega**bytes** per second. A lot slower than it sounds, since 40Mbps = 5MBps.

Video Resources

To help you understand the procedures and concepts explored in this book, we have developed some video resources and app demos for you to use, as you work through the book.

As well as the video resources, you'll also find some downloadable files and samples for exercises that appear in the book.

To find the resources, open your web browser and navigate to the following website

elluminetpress.com/hw

Do not use a search engine, type the website into the address field at the top of the browser window.

At the beginning of each chapter, you'll find a website that contains the resources for that chapter.

Using the Videos

When you open the link to the video resources, you'll see a thumbnail list at the bottom. Click the images to open the sections.

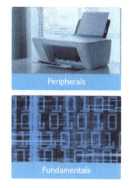

Click on the thumbnail for the particular video you want to watch. Most videos are between 30 and 60 seconds outlining the procedure, others are a bit longer. When the video is playing, hover your mouse over the video and you'll see some controls...

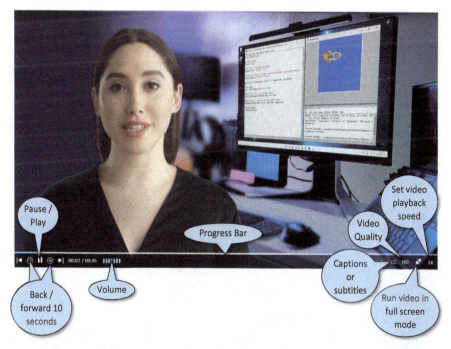

You'll find various controls along the bottom of the video window. Here you can start/stop, go back/forward 10 seconds, add captions, and run the video in full screen.

File Resources

You'll find various cheat sheets, info and PowerPoint files in this section.

To save the files into your computer, right click on the icons above and select 'download linked file as'.

In the dialog box that appears, select the folder you want to save the download into - use 'documents'.

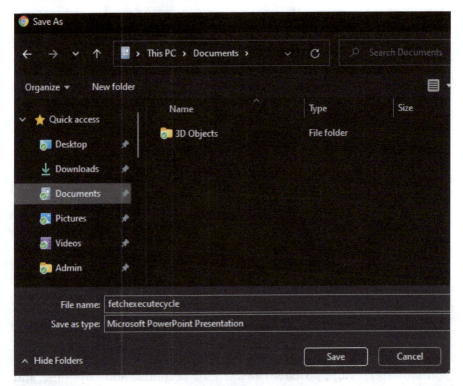

Click 'save'.

Once you have downloaded the file, go to file explorer and navigate to your documents folder. Here, you'll find the downloaded files.

Double click the file to open. You'll need PowerPoint installed on your machine for this to work.

You'll also find additional resources under the 'cheat sheet' section.

Cheat Sheets

Click on the icons below...

Motherboard Labelled

Download these in the same way as before.

Finally, at the bottom of the resources page, you'll see a list of relevant text books.

Relevant Textbooks

Click on the icons below to download the files.

Computer Jargon

Essential Computer Hardware

Scanning the Codes

At the beginning of each chapter, you'll a QR code you can scan with your phone to access additional resources, files and videos.

iPhone

To scan the code with your iPhone/iPad, open the camera app.

Frame the code in the middle of the screen. Tap on the website popup at the top.

Android

To scan the code with your phone or tablet, open the camera app.

Frame the code in the middle of the screen. Tap on the website popup at the top.

If it doesn't scan, turn on 'Scan QR codes'. To do this, tap the settings icon on the top left. Turn on 'scan QR codes'.

If the setting isn't there, you'll need to download a QR Code scanner. Open the Google Play Store, then search for "QR Code Scanner".

Index

Index

Index

Index

X

Z

SOMETHING NOT COVERED?

We want to create the best possible resources to help you learn and get things done, so if we've missed anything out, then please get in touch using the links below and let us know. Thanks.

 office@elluminetpress.com

 elluminetpress.com/feedback

www.ingramcontent.com/pod-product-compliance
Lightning Source LLC
Chambersburg PA
CBHW071115050326
40690CB00008B/1227